STILL COMMON SENSE

RODGER CARLYLE

This is a work of non-fiction.

STILL COMMON SENSE. Copyright © 2022 by Rodger Carlyle.

Published in the United States by Verity Books, an imprint of Comsult, LLC.

All rights reserved. Except for brief passages except quoted in newspaper, magazine, radio, television or online reviews, no portion of this book may be reproduced, distributed, or transmitted in any form or by any means, electronic or mechanical including photocopying, recording, or information storage or retrieval systems without the prior written permission of the author and/or Comsult, LLC.

First published in 2022.

ISBN 978-1-7379497-4-9 (e-book)
ISBN 978-1-7379497-1-8 (paperback)

*"Do I not destroy my enemies when
I make them my friend?"*

—Abraham Lincoln

This book is dedicated to sharing with you the economic, historical, legal, and societal beliefs that make up what I call truth. Your interpretation of the same components is every bit as valid to your truths. While I hope to expose you to some different beliefs, some different historical facts, what I hope for the most is that you can see that what I want in America is similar to what you want.

"Fight for the things that you care about. But do it in a way that will lead others to join you."

—Ruth Bader Ginsburg

PREFACE

WHY I WROTE THIS BOOK...THE COLLISION OF THINKING AND FEELING

Brothers and sisters not talking. Parents and their kids stressing over beliefs. Politicians afraid to work out their differences. Massive tax increases that seem to do nothing. Spending and debt that exceed what was needed to win World War II. Your media is all propaganda, yours is all lies. Trump is saving the country. No Trump is destroying the nation. Racist, you are destroying the planet. Socialist, go back to work. I'm right, you're wrong. You rich business owners just don't understand what it's like to be a worker.

Two men were talking about what could be done to bridge the liberal-conservative divide. The conversation wasn't about promoting one side or the other, rather they were concerned that the fraying edges of society were slowly tearing at the center. Each had experienced difficult conversations in the past few days. Employees, friends, even relatives were angry, but when asked why, didn't have any clear explanation. It's just not fair isn't much of a starting point for a discussion. The fair response had been part of conversations between the business community and employees for years. Diversity, equity, and inclusion on one hand. Opportunity, obligation, and commitment on the other. Profits keep the doors open and provide the capital to grow. Profits are just taking money out of the pockets of the workers. It seemed these conversations were between people living in parallel worlds.

The men bumped into each other over the years serving each other's business growth by providing goods and services. Both had been stung by businesspeople who failed to live up to their commitments, and employees who believed having a job didn't mean doing the job. Beyond any other connection, both had started with next to nothing and built successful companies. Both were white, and to many that meant that the door to success was already open for them.

One, Dave, is a construction executive with business interests in multiple states. The other an author who spent years in the business world before a battle with a rare cancer made it clear that it was time to pursue the career he'd always wanted. One is a Republican deeply engaged in his church. The other, the author, is an independent who is never closer to God than when sitting by a clear running river. Both are focused on family and the community. Both moved away from their home states to seek greater opportunity. Both are pilots and find that outdoor activities are the perfect release needed from intense careers.

Over the months, these men continued the conversation with other men and women, liberal and conservative. Only one common theme emerged, everyone was unhappy.

We start with this brief profile to be clear and honest about the origins of this book. All of us share a deep concern about where the country is heading and about how divided we have become. To the two friends, the divide seems to be more about process than final results. Perhaps that is because our educational backgrounds emphasize process. One of us is a science major with an emphasis on chemistry and biology and the other a political science major with emphasis in political economics and language.

In both fields of study there are absolutes based on facts, but way more unknowns than knowns. **Keep that thought in mind, more unknowns than knowns.**

Shining a light onto the unknowns is critical to both fields. Certain biological behaviors, for example among animals, are repetitive enough and consistent enough to be labeled truths. Yet one of the critical pieces of scientific research is to study exceptions. Political Science focuses on human interaction and much of that is also predictable. Political doctrine focuses on how man interacts with others in a defined world. Yet at times the defined world turns upside down.

For example, in much of today's discourse, success is labeled destructive; successful people accumulating wealth are evil. Those struggling to better themselves, lacking skills and specific talents are too often labeled lazy. Where the free speech movement of the 1970's treasured differences and debate, with universities creating areas where people could argue vast differences in opinion, today speech is controlled or even canceled if it makes anyone uncomfortable. In political discourse, those we disagree with are no longer just incorrect, they are stupid or to those on the left, racist and on the right, pariahs. How do we ever find solutions that will be accepted by both sides as long as we all can't get passed labels and name calling. These tendencies are exacerbated by media and social media who emphasize and even create conflict to generate followers. One side is becoming immune to the attacks, while the other finds itself wrapped up in fear. Fear is a critical response to imminent danger; it keeps us alive. But fear over issues and activities that have a minimal chance of ever affecting a person cripples their ability to deal with issues rationally.

In a recent get together the author found himself surrounded by that fear. Fear that COVID would be the death of participants or loved ones. Fear of what the media labeled racist social structure that made some victims and others perpetrators just because of their skin. Fear of anyone who owned a gun. When discussing the get together with a conservative friend, her response was to discredit each of these feelings, but that does not help alleviate the concerns of those living in fear, for those concerns have become their truth.

> **"Fear is a reaction; courage is a decision."**
> **—Winston Churchill**

The author began looking at the overly simplified platitudes, slogans, and memes popular today. This research began as our community began discussing an upcoming political race for a congressional seat. In the race, a long seated Republican incumbent was facing challenges from right and left. On the right is a young man, from the family of a former Blue Dog Democratic congressman. (Blue Dog here means a traditional labor oriented, national security conscious, Democrat who believes in Free Enterprise and the Constitution and fights to make sure working men and women share in its bounty.) He has labeled a sitting congressman who has been reelected as a Republican more than a dozen times as an apologist of the liberal movement. The congressman's failures included supporting the economy of this state. On the left is a sitting city assembly member who accuses the challenger from the right of, "more extreme right-wing messaging." Adding "That kind of thinking cannot be the center of this campaign. We can't drive more to the right, or we're going to fall off the edge of the flat world." Really, just because someone has different political views, they are pre-renaissance dupes.

This same kind of rhetoric is exploding across the country. It takes little for some to be negatively labeled as socialists and communists. Those who come from the other extreme consider anyone who disagrees with them uneducated, anti-science, racist Neanderthals. Here are a few of our most concerning slogans.

LEFT	RIGHT
White Male Privilege	White Power
Pro Choice	Pro Life
"My fear is that if North Korea nukes us, Trump is going to get us into a war."	In Africa some idiot shoots a lion and it's the Shooter's fault; in America one person shoots another and it's the gun's fault.
Basket of Deplorables	LIBERALS: people waiting on someone to tell them what to be offended about next.
Question: What do you call 242 Republicans in one house? Answer: Useless	I just love being cussed out and bullied by Leftists for not being as tolerant as they are.
The only people who don't accept the theory of evolution are those who have not yet themselves begun the process.	It's nuts; you have to show your vaccination card to get into a restaurant, but it's impossible to ask for ID when voting.
I wish more people cared about the earth as much as they care about who they believe created it.	Snowflake
GOP = greed over people	Let's go Brandon

Political sloganeering has been part of American political campaigns since the time of the founding fathers. Some slogans have been nuts. For example, in 1928, Al Smith, Democrat, ran for President on the slogan, "let your wet dreams come true." He was speaking about ending prohibition, but the slogan was not well received. He lost, and the slogan took on new meaning over the decades. Today sloganeering has become part of everyday life. Campaigns never end. It appears that social media would dry up without the vitriol. (Just had the thought, maybe that would be just fine.) And the nastiness and demeaning of the 'other side' just inflames the public. With that said, our research shows that much of the disagreement stems from three issues.

- Few people today really know why, on what issues, with which concerns and limitations the nation was founded. Students today learn what the Constitution is, even that it replaced the weak 'articles of confederation.' But they do not learn how applies to society or even to themselves; what does liberty mean to me.

- Liberals think we should be equal at the finish line, while conservatives think we should be equal at the starting line. People do not understand the basics of the economy.

- Much of what we now call history has become a debate that begins with favored conclusions and then sorts through what happened in the past to find only those moments that prove that conclusion. What each of us learns from almost any moment in history is open to interpretation. But history itself is not there for us to like or dislike, it is there to learn from.

Your tribe has always hurt my tribe. Your tribe is lazy. All your tribe cares about is money.

Just nuts.

With this opening, I set out to write this book, a student of my own educational disciplines and of American history, to see if I could do anything that addressed the naivety and vitriol of America today. I would write the book while Dave offered support, scientific background, and criticism. The PhDs on both sides write a book read by people who already believe what they believe, get interviewed the next week and change no opinions. Neither of us work for Fox News or OAN. Neither of us is enamored by Facebook, CNN, or MSNBC. Instead, we are what we believe the nation needs most, fairly common men. People whose observations and study are of other regular citizens. All of the time and energy to write this book is the author's, with no compensation from groups trying to prove anything. To some who start reading, the tone of this book may seem politically charged. It is. I am personally deeply concerned about where the country is heading but acknowledge that the issues are complex and there is strong emotion on each side. The book contains a lot of facts, including a lot of detail on society. It has all been checked and double checked, but I am not writing as an academic expert, so those of you who might question sections of the book should feel free to research those issues yourself. I am not including citations since one of the main goals of this project is to entice those with strong feelings to dig a little deeper.

My own bias will come through in the manuscript. I have enough grey hair to have lived through the Civil Rights Turmoil of the 1960's, the anti-war turmoil of the 1970's, the energy crises of the Arab Oil embargo and three wars. I have no friends who have made no mistakes, none who don't have skeletons in their closet. America is and will always be one of my best friends and like my human friends it has a checkered past but somehow always improved.

Thinking through how to open this book, the author was constantly drawn to the book, *Common Sense*, by Thomas Paine, a short pamphlet printed in the 1770's. In *Common Sense*, Paine laid out the argument for the creation of the United States of America. In this book, I lay out why those reasons are still valid and why the social-economic-political model laid out two and a half centuries ago is still the best model to remedy todays differences. But that is only valid if you know the model and if you apply it equally and persistently across the country. It is only true if we all agree about what needs fixing and quit fighting about how to fix it.

I'd like to call those who embrace the findings, NATURAL AMERICANS; a description that came from Dave. That doesn't mean that there will not be other ideas, only that the people who founded the nation, built the nation, then fought for its very existence and sacrificed for it created a model that will work for all of us. So why isn't it as effective today as in the past? Bluntly, because we quit following it. In an era of instant gratification, we have lost our patience, lost an awareness that social and economic trends are not as simple as posting inflaming social media posts and getting followers. Nor is it as simple as discrediting others because they don't look like us.

One final disclosure before we launch *Still Common Sense*. In the first year after it was founded, the Smithsonian Museum of Black History put on its website what they called, ASPECTS AND ASSUMPTIONS OF WHITENESS AND WHITE CULTURE.

This post was to layout the ways white people and their traditions are now considered standard practices in the United States, somehow hurting people of color. Listed among the White Aspects are:

RUGGED INDIVIDUALISM - The individual is the primary unit; Self-reliance; independence and autonomy highly valued and rewarded; individuals assumed to be in control of their environment.

FAMILY STRUCTURE - The nuclear family: father, mother, children is the ideal social unit; Husband is the primary breadwinner and head of household; Wife is homemaker and subordinate to the husband; Children should be independent

EMPHASIS ON SCIENTIFIC METHOD - Objective, rational linear thinking; cause and effect relationships; quantitative emphasis.

HISTORY - Based on Northern European immigrant experience in the United States; heavy focus on the British Empire; the primacy of Western (Greek, Roman) and Judeo-Christian tradition.

PROTESTANT WORK ETHIC - Hard work is the key to

success; work before play; if you didn't meet your goals, you didn't work hard enough.

The website went on to discuss religion, status, power and authority, future orientation, time, aesthetics, holidays, and justice. Each of these sections addresses additional aspects of what they call Whiteness. For example, under future orientation, it lists, "plan for the future; delayed gratification; progress is always best; tomorrow will be better." The museum's presentation was a bit dated.

I include this because, except for the section on family structure, where the author's wife would certainly "revise" the hypothesis, the rest of the outline largely describes how the author has lived his life. Whether it is from culture and habits of their own ethnic groups or what society now calls "Cultural Appropriation," it is how most Americans live their lives.

That term, cultural appropriation, to me, is an oxymoron in a nation and society that is built on people from all over the world and every ethnicity. How crazy to criticize fellow citizens for adopting, treasuring, and displaying the cultures of fellow citizens. You won't see me trashing the bicameral legislative system drawn from Native Americans, R&B, belief in faith, Blues and resilience from Black Americans, Sushi, intense belief in discipline and belief in education from Asian Americans. My Latina wife, a city girl, and I listen to Carlos Santana and Linda Ronstadt with our Tacos. We have one room in our home she calls the Barrio Art Gallery, with art from modern Latin artists. I love it and she appreciates our den with Western wildlife art. We love New Orleans because it is a true melting pot. Oh, and we do those White things noted earlier.

I want you to know where this book is coming from. But in order to really evaluate the current social construct, I underwrote a survey looking for the opinions of other Americans, paying special attention to those who label themselves differently. Most would call me moderately conservative or Libertarian. The results of that survey are in chapter one of the book.

I am Rodger, a political scientist, businessman and writer. I've spent years studying American and world political history. I've worked in countries across the globe, and write historical fiction, usually based on some screwup or miscalculation that was covered up by the powerful. I am dumbfounded by watching how the very things that have made America successful are now under attack. Two favorite quotations fit here:

> **"People have to think, that's not to agree or disagree, that's voting."**
>
> –Robert Frost

> **"Honest disagreement is often a good sign of progress."**
>
> –Mahatma Gandhi

Both Dave and I were surprised to find that the other was contemplating a book. Rodger was focused on economic, social, and political disagreement but was struggling to find a single unifying human model as an explanation. Dave had been gathering notes for years on what he believed were natural human traits, truths that explained both successful enterprise and damaging behavior. Both believed that American citizens (and other people) have a responsibility to first do no harm to their fellow citizens. Both believe that society only works if we live up to our agreements with others. Both believe the American Dream is alive and well but acknowledge that a lot of citizens don't even understand that term. The USA was the first nation on earth that was conceived purely on the principles of individual liberty and freedom. But with great freedom and liberty, comes great responsibility.

It took several conversations to realize that what Dave referred to as the Natural American, a set of behaviors and responsibilities, were just the unifying human model Rodger was looking for. It might work as a model for at least understanding our differences. America was born of conflict. It has never had a period where there was not substantial political disagreement. That is a critical difference to countries where people are manipulated or bluntly told what to do, to think. I write this as the Ukraine war rages, but my Russian friends, almost all of which have friends and relatives in Ukraine are told and believe that the war is about rooting out Nazis. The government and media are only allowed to tell the people what they want the public to hear. There has never been a time when American's didn't believe we have more in common than differences, until now. This book was born.

"If you feel pain, you are alive. If you feel other people's pain, you are a human being."

–Leo Tolstoy

1

CITIZEN SURVEY ON AMERICAN ECONOMIC AND SOCIAL ISSUES

A SURVEY AND meeting with Melody, a passionate, liberal person.
What the author had trouble wrapping his mind around, was that so much of the liberal/progressive media was so angry, so determined to reinvent America and so determined to blame especially those who are conservatives. My question, blame them for what? Where was America failing? How do conservative beliefs and values contribute to that failure? What is racist about the color of any person's skin? Was Martin Luther King wrong when he spoke to equality of men? How is the American economic system responsible for poverty? Why is equity for all superior to growing success for all?

Conservative media warped its message by justifying the behavior of hate groups and individuals. There is no justification for hate. Like the other side, much of their commentary has become "what I feel" instead of "what I know." Both sides manipulate their audience to promote an agenda, improve ratings, and attract revenues. Gone are the days of reporting an incident without labeling someone. The people who made American Media News the envy of the world must be rolling over in their graves,

The author commissioned a 20-question survey to get some general understanding of how the public, who described themselves as progressive or liberal, really understand and feel about America, its founding documents, its economic system, economic classes, and their responsibilities. I used this tool as the liberals I attempted to have a conversation with refused to discuss their views if they felt our beliefs differed. The author was obviously uncaring and blind to victims.

I surveyed self-described conservatives by phone. They talked freely, but even some business colleagues shook when they found that we had different beliefs. The author was obviously an apologist.

Boy were both sides wrong.

I deliberately mixed up historic, economic, and social questions to avoid respondents offering hyped policy instead of their personal views. I guaranteed that the responses would be confidential and stripped of names before tabulation. I released the survey in phases, to look at diverse groups. (For example, we sent one batch to only elected officials.) We offered the earliest respondents a gift certificate to either Amazon or Barnes & Noble Booksellers as a reward for prompt responses. I planned to discard any responses that were profane or demeaning and received none. (I deliberately did not include media personalities.)

In order to guarantee anonymity, I hired out the tabulation, in fact, I haven't even asked for how many respondents, from which groups, responded. The tabulators were paid in cash to compile the results. Their reports did not include the names of the tabulators.

The survey asked that the respondents be as concise as they could in their answers. Some offered one or two sentence answers. Others felt a need to explain their responses. From the compilation, I created a composite answer, seeking midpoints in the liberal responses, which turned out to be a relatively simple task as so many of the responses were common. Most of the responses could have been picked from waves of comments on social media.

Below are the questions and composite answers to the progressive survey.

Composite Answers

1. HOW DO YOU VIEW YOUR POLITICAL BELIEFS?

    80% of the respondents defined themselves as "liberal or left leaning," while 20% chose not to say.

2. MANY PEOPLE BELIEVE THAT AMERICA IS AN EXCEPTIONAL COUNTRY. HOW WOULD YOU DESCRIBE IT?

    "Beautiful, diverse, immature, confused. Exceptional in some individuals have more rights than others. America is both exceptional in the sense that there never has been nor ever will be any country quite like it, and nothing special in that the same is true for every country."

3. DESCRIBE YOUR UNDERSTANDING AND FEELINGS ABOUT CAPITALISM.

    "I don't have a deep understanding of capitalism. Money has become the God of capitalists. Our job is to help each other, not profit off each other."

4. WHAT IS THE ROLE OF THE CONSTITUTION TODAY?

    "I don't know for sure. Maybe it is the nation's book of rules. People can change it, but it must be done legally. Still too many people feel 'exceptional', and the antiquated

Constitution represents an outdated fixed mindset that is preventing the country from progressing."

5. WHAT IS WEALTH?

   "An abundance, more than you really need, of material things; or to others contentment from friends, health, and enjoyment of nature."

6. WHAT IS SOCIAL JUSTICE AND YOUR RESPONSIBILITY TOWARDS IT?

   "Social Justice is evenly distributed wealth, opportunities, and privilege; it is the counterforce to oppression and tyranny. My responsibility is to strive for a more perfect union, not just those with wealth, power and who look, or worship like me."

7. WHAT IS ECONOMIC JUSTICE AND YOUR RESPONSIBILITY TOWARDS IT?

   "Outlaw people inheriting the debt or wealth of their predecessors. Remove unjust barriers, and historic systems that have not adapted to contemporary society. Make sure financial and educational opportunities are fair."

8. IS RACIAL EQUALITY AND ECONOMIC JUSTICE BETTER OR WORSE THAN 50 YEARS AGO?

   80% of the respondents said better, while 20% said worse.

9. HOW DO YOU HELP THE NATION'S ECONOMY?

   "Spending my money, mostly local and paying my taxes. I advocate for higher wages and benefits from employers and work within the community, especially with younger people and promote healthy investment choices."

10. WHAT IS A CITIZEN? WHAT IS YOUR DEFINITION OF A 'REAL AMERICAN?'

   "A citizen is someone born in the USA or who has passed a citizenship test. A Real American follows the laws and respects the rights of others. They love America, accepting the great things, work to remedy its downfalls, and ensure America adapts to the times."

11. IS GREAT INDIVIDUAL OR FAMILY WEALTH GOOD OR BAD FOR SOCIETY?

   60% of the respondents feel wealth is bad, while 40% said it was good.

12. HOW DOES ONE IMPROVE THEIR PERSONAL OR FAMILY FINANCIAL SITUATION?

   "Can that still be done today? Beats me, no seriously, get an education or skilled trade since those on minimum wage work their butts off and can't support a family. Maybe get a financial planner or win a contest or a lawsuit. Work hard, make smart choices and look for help if you need it. Some do not have the educational physical or mental ability to improve their situation."

13. SOME JUDGES BELIEVE THEY NEED TO REINTERPRET THE CONSTITUTION. OTHERS BELIEVE THAT IF THE CONSTITUTION NEEDS REVISING IT SHOULD GO THROUGH THE AMMENDMENT PROCESS. WHAT ARE YOUR THOUGHTS?

   "The evolution of society requires reinterpretation of the Constitution, and each new look should not require an amendment. However, even if the Constitution contains antiquated concepts, it is the one legal consistent document and should not be open to individual interpretation."

14. WHICH COMES FIRST, EQUALITY OR FREEDOM?

    80% of respondents named equality and 20% said freedom.

15. WHICH COMES FIRST, RIGHTS OR OBLIGATIONS?

    60% of respondents said obligations, while 40% said rights.

16. WHICH COMES FIRST, PRIVILEGES OR RESPONSIBILITY?

    100% of respondents said responsibility.

17. WEALTHY SOCIETIES WITH MORE LIESURE TIME PRODUCE MORE ART, MUSIC, AND LITERATURE. IS THIS GOOD?

    100% of the respondents said yes.

18. WHAT NATURAL LAWS INFLUENCE OR CONTROL THE BEHAVIOR OF MAN?

    "Maybe belonging to a tribe, protecting oneself and one's resources. Or maybe simply eating, breathing, sleeping and the additional needs defined by our consciousness and interpersonal relationships."

19. SOCIALISM SPEAKS TO DIVIDING PRODUCTION MORE EQUITABLY. IS THIS A GOOD MODEL? WHY?

    "Generally, for medicine and education it is probably good. Maybe CEOs should not make insane pay and excess could go to workers. But I'm torn between share and share alike and realizing some work at more difficult jobs and work harder and have prepared more and it would not be fair to pay them the same."

20. WHAT IS THE DIFFERENCE BETWEEN 'ACTIONS BASED ON THINKING' VERSUS 'ACTIONS BASED ON FEELING?'

"Thinking actions would be based on facts, but only as gained from reliable sources. Feeling actions often are based on our personal experiences and may be objective or biased. Often decisions based on feelings lead us to jump to conclusions or are just emotional responses. You need to think before you act."

I tried to conduct an earlier survey by phone, but the answers were so emotionally charged that a question like "which comes first, equality or freedom," would elicit an answer like, "if you can't see that equality is more important, there is no hope." So, I went to our written questionnaire to solicit personal answers to how people really feel and not how they think we should feel.

While the survey was being conducted, I did a voice survey of conservatives. As in the solicitation list for liberal input, I again deleted media. Again, the responses were similar. Both liberals and conservatives are fairly locked in on their views. Overall, what I learned from the responses was that the conservatives and the liberals talk past each other, they don't even agree on common definitions. Conservatives seemed to have a better grasp of the nation's founding, documents, and actions. (By definition, conservative thinkers tend to rely on the past to craft their beliefs.)

The liberals were critical of perceived current situations and problems. Progressive thinking looks at today's issues and wonder why they still exist. Some were openly hostile toward the founding fathers, evaluating them through the screen of today's values.

(It is inconceivable to them that someone who had ever owned slaves could be a serious supporter of individual liberty.) The conservatives tended to have relatively simple ideas on problems and solutions. The liberal responses tended to reveal an impatience for solutions with few specifics. Conservatives tended to see few structural problems in our current society, while liberals appeared willing to see primarily institutional problems and were quick to assign blame. Liberals wanted someone, preferably government to fix problems, while conservatives asserted that only the people can do that. Remember the earlier observation, that there are more unknowns than knowns. Neither progressive nor conservatives discussed unknowns. Both were locked in by what they already know and weren't particularly interested in exploring unknowns.

One other thing surprised me from the survey of elected officials. On the conservative side, some granted a few minutes of telephone time to gain a brief understanding of their views. None wanted to complete a survey. None of the liberal leaning elected officials wanted to talk or return the online survey. Instead, we got feedback such as, "By allowing the two-party system to prevail, we set ourselves up for this;" and, "We will always have a divide…." Not much encouragement there.

So, the survey of liberal views is made up of common citizens, views solicited from a significant range of age groups and careers. I was interested in the responses, not a policy debate, and only wanted answers from those willing to offer personal responses.

From their responses, I developed consensus answers and from that hereby attributed them to our liberal avatar, Melody. What do we mean by liberal Avatar? The book is set up to reflect a conversation between myself one progressive/liberal person, a composite of those surveyed: an Avatar. I chose a woman Avatar as the women in the survey were by far more willing to discuss their personal views than the men, who generally just parroted talking points. As you read this, remember that Melody is just a name for an Avatar, a composite person. If you are concerned about a liberal woman being chosen to represent those views, then feel free to change the Avatar's name to Lawrence or Tim. But in the survey, women provided more concise and well thought out responses than the men.

I want to listen to a concern and conduct a one-to-one conversation. I will break these conversations into four sections. First, a conversation about the American economy; (economic issues including taxation were the primary fuel for the American Revolution and current equality concerns.) Second, a discussion of history both before European presence in North America and up until the present. Third, I set out to openly discuss both historic and present societal pressures and the law. In the fourth section, I will attempt to lay out a Unifying Philosophy; that is a set of terms with agreed upon definitions, that can be applied to any set of facts or situation to at least allow us a civil discussion. These aren't rules, rather some ideas on how we avoid wasting time and energy on settled issues, (historical issues that cannot be changed, like slavery was bad) and focus on making lives better.

From this point forward, I would like to thank Melody for being part of this book and thank all of you who make up Melody for your responses. You all made your point and I acknowledge your concerns. I heard you.

Here is what I heard. Melody told me that she really doesn't understand how to go about improving her personal or family financial situation or that of others. She is focused on working hard, and making smart choices, and believes education helps. She commented on minimum wage issues and recognized that entry level pay today is inadequate to support a family. Maybe winning a lawsuit or hiring a financial planner helps. As to how she helps the economy as a whole, well she spends money, tries to spend it locally and promotes advocacy for higher wages and benefits especially among younger people. Melody is concerned that some people, because of mental or physical difficulties, may not be able to earn a living on their own. **It** isn't fair.

On the subject of wealth, Melody defined wealth as more than one's need of material things or other contentments. Sixty percent of the time, she felt that great individual or family wealth is bad for society, and yet felt that wealth creates the ability to produce more art, music, and literature, which she stated was very important. She felt that families passing on wealth to their children was generally a bad thing. Wealthy people only became wealthy by taking from less privileged.

When asked about capitalism versus socialism, Melody offered a mixed bag of thoughts. Generally, she acknowledged that she doesn't really understand capitalism. She finds that capitalists are focused on money instead of taking care of their fellow man. Her understanding of socialism is also limited, although she thinks it is a good idea for, maybe medicine and education. Here she is focused on CEO pay as basically unfair, but still believes that certain jobs, utilizing certain education or training are worth more than others especially those requiring more work. Government should take more from the wealthy, but how that might work is a question.

In general, her thoughts go quickly to what is fair. She believes that unjust barriers and historic systems that do not reflect contemporary society, need to be dismantled while we refocus on financial and educational opportunities for all.

In chapter five and six, I tackle the foundations of our social system, economic system, and government through a discussion of history. Melody seems to feel that those old white gentlemen who signed the Declaration of Independence, fought in the Revolutionary War, created the U.S. Constitution would be out of step with today's world and values. While most of the time she feels economic justice has improved over the last half century, sometimes she is disappointed. She described the nation as beautiful, diverse, immature, and confused. She sees our history as built around a concept of protecting the rights of some while limiting the rights of others. She is concerned about inequity. Her comment that there is no other country quite like America, but it's nothing special in that the same is true for every country, indicates that she sees nothing really exceptional in the country.

In Chapter 7, I want to discuss our society under the law with Melody. Her views on The Constitution indicate that she isn't quite sure what the role of the document is today. She sees it as a book of rules that are subject to reinterpretation but at the same time believes that any changes must be done legally through the amendment process. (Conservatives tend to accept societal rules and focus on working within them for needed change.)

Her understanding is based on a strong belief that equality is more important than freedom. To many, people feel 'exceptional' because the antiquated Constitution represents an outdated fixed mindset that is preventing the country from progressing. A more perfect union would be one where privilege extends to all, not just those with wealth and power or who look… look what? Look white or live in big homes, or are athletes or performers, she's not sure.

Melody generally believes that obligations come before rights but not always, in fact, the term rights is pervasive in most of her comments. Responsibilities always comes before privileges. She believes that there are natural laws that control man's behavior such as belonging to a tribe, or protecting yourself, or your resources. We all need to eat and breath and sleep, but our consciousness and interpersonal relationships also are critical to our behavior. She believes actions need to be based on critical thinking backed up by facts. Too often, decisions based on feelings lead to jumping to conclusions. I also believe there are controlling natural laws.

In summary, Melody is really critical of America, of society, but doesn't really understand why the nation is as it is. She fervently believes that things can be better with greater opportunity for all. Melody would choose two words that describe her concerns, equality and fair.

First, I support and encourage Melody in her concerns for

others. I agree that things can be better for her and others. America's citizens need to seize greater opportunity for all. The nation was conceived on the concept of liberty and equal rights for all. Capitalists <u>are</u> focused on money. The Constitution is a 'book of rules' and more, it lays out the guiding principles for the American society. I agree with Melody's wide perception that things are not right in America.

With that opening, I also believe that things are not all wrong with America. Many of Melody's concerns stem from three areas. First, she sees The Constitution, America's book of rules as out of step with current society, needing either revision or reinterpreting. I will have a conversation with Melody about that Constitution, believing that a lot of things might be better if we actually followed the Constitution again. Second, Melody looks at inequity as a negative. Here again, I would like to discuss the differences between equity and equal rights, and how obligation plays into that thought. Third, Melody sees the economy as unfair, with exceptional wealth for some and poverty for others. Here I believe that much of the problem lies in how few of America's citizens even understand our economic system. It is no longer taught in school; rather it has been replaced with simple sloganeering. Economic issues are complex, but how the system works is not. (As stated, this educational failure is an absolute, but I know that across the country many teachers still offer comparative economic study, that is if the lesson police, the curriculum coordinators in their schools allow it.) Many educators struggle to promote career choices with dirty fingernails. I understand Melody's focus on equality and fair but believe that before either of these can become the national norm, the people of this country need to focus on liberty and opportunity.

Moving into the discussion; the American economy has created the highest overall standard of living in the world. This is remarkable as it is the only major economy built around a really diverse population. All other highly successful economies are in countries with mostly homogenic populations with common history and language, for example Japan and Sweden. I want to have a direct conversation about that economy; how American history and its founding created a model for success and how we have reinterpreted that history to our detriment. Were traditional cultures trampled along the way, for example native American, yes. Did they evolve, yes. Are they part of who we are now, yes. American society and our legal system create a blueprint for success if we all just understood it. It also offers opportunity to redress injustice.

But before I can move to those discussions, Melody should know what I consider is the American success story. It is the story of the founding and building of a remarkable nation. It is the story of individuals, I'll call them Natural Americans, who built a nation, sometimes directing government to help, but more often in spite of government. It is an ongoing story, not one that history will ever call complete. It is the story of individual people not of institutions. It is her story and mine, ours. Let's see how, together, we can improve this work in progress and make a better America.

You cannot bring about prosperity by discouraging thrift.
You cannot strengthen the weak by weakening the strong.
You cannot help little men by tearing down big men.
*You cannot lift the wage earner by
pulling down the wage payer.*
You cannot help the poor by destroying the rich.
You cannot establish sound security on borrowed money.
*You cannot further the brotherhood of
man by inciting class hatred.*
*You cannot keep out of trouble by
spending more than you earn.*
*You cannot build character and courage by
destroying men's initiative and independence.*
*And you cannot help men permanently by doing for
them what they can and should do for themselves.*

—Abraham Lincoln

2

THE NATURAL AMERICAN

A discussion about Natural Americans and their belief system

As noted in the preface, Dave has developed what he calls a theory of Natural Americans. As he began explaining it to me, he used several personal stories, and I believe that is a good way to open this section. As you read this section, ask yourself, does this apply to me?

Here is Dave's foundation story.

"Chest puffed, feet spread, his five-year-old finger stabbing up toward the smirking face of his towering cousin, he snarled, YOU ARE NOT THE BOSS OF ME. Simple, resolute, and matter of fact.

My boy was never taught this but there it was, a deep and thorough knowledge that he owned himself and he alone would determine what was in his best interest, at least until he crossed an out of bounds line that would lead to punishment.

He was never given a menu to choose his own behavioral characteristics. That was done for him through generations of his ancestors, men and women who stuck their fingers in the face of kings and emperors, nobility, dictators and declared to them, YOU ARE NOT THE BOSS OF ME. Nobody had ever threatened him or encouraged fear of being his own boss.

These are our ancestors, some already here and many more who came to America for freedom. They left tribalism and feudalism behind seeking freedom. Freedom to worship as they saw fit and to own property, to prosper and be secure in the fruits of their own labor. Where no one else would be the boss of them they built the greatest nation in world history."

This is one of the precepts of how we might define a Natural American. A Natural American believes that he or she is an independent critical piece of what makes this country work. They believe that all they have to offer is their time (infusing time with their knowledge, critical thinking, and physical ability), and they alone own that time.

The creation of America was not smooth; in fact, it was more like dragging a wooden sled over a boulder field. Dozens of old beliefs, cultural and social institutions were discarded or destroyed. Bits and pieces of those same old beliefs, culture and social institutions were molded together into a new society. Unfortunately, enslaved people, did not grow up poking their finger in the chests of others, crying, 'you don't own me.' (I deeply believe they thought that.) Their ability and willingness to own themselves is a checkered tale. But throughout that history, they like all Natural Americans, knew the truth. Blood was shed, traditions trampled, people fought and died. But eventually, the warring opponents became one nation, made up of diverse people. We can and should learn from our history, even mistakes, but you can never go back.

This resonated with me. I write Historical Fiction, with a clear aversion to superheroes. In a real-world crisis, how long are we going to wait around for some superhero to ride in on a white horse and save us? Most of America's great battles and conflicts were won by ordinary men and women who found themselves in extraordinary circumstances and refused to fail. I never thought of giving them a name, but Natural American works. It sure as hell isn't Politicians.

Below is Dave's biological battle story.

"In all the universe, amongst trillions of stars and galaxies all we really know of life exists here on earth. A fragile film of life, maybe from the depts of the deepest sea to 16,000 feet above those seas. Like mist on a marble in the grand picture of our galaxy.

Ask a bunch of first graders the difference between living and non-living things and the first thing they'll say is living things move around. Then they'll think about plants and realize living things eat and drink and die. Ask a wizened 80-year-old grandmother what the most important thing about being alive is and she will say her grandkids.

It could be said that an egg reproduces itself by making a bird. It could also be said that genes reproduce themselves by growing living things. They are very, very, selfish and all they care about is reproducing themselves no matter what it takes. From a virus to a human and everything in between reproducing one's self is the essence of their existence. It is a trait that is hardwired into the DNA of every species and every viable individual on Earth.

For an individual of any species to sustain its own life and successfully reproduce, it will always need territory. I use the term as interchangeable with critical resources or wealth. Having territory is the difference between life and death, existence, and extinction. Every living thing needs it and will fight to the death to get it.

Some symbiotic relationships between individuals of any one species, or between different species are often offset by battle. Plants battle for their territory of sunlight, water, minerals, and nutrients. Many have devised methods of poisoning their competing neighbors with chemicals like cyanide. Symbiotic groups battle other symbiotic groups, seeking to exploit every niche in the ecosystem. Members of the same species compete with each other the most since they need exactly the same resources.

The single greatest goal of every individual organism is to gain the most territory (resources) with the least amount of effort and cost to itself in order to raise offspring who in turn raise offspring. Every normal parent wants a better life for their children and grandchildren. The instinct to gain wealth is ultimately on behalf of their children.

Among most species, other than the laws of physics, there are no rules between members of the same species in the fight for resources. Everything on earth acknowledges the law of gravity. Gravity is the most honest, most reliable, and most honorable force in the universe. It's always there, it never quits and with absolutely no exception governs the behavior of individuals every second or their conception, birth, life, death, and decomposition. Like gravity, there are other natural truths, the earth rotates so that the sun 'rises' in the east; the sun is the primary source of all energy on earth and so on. The one clear natural law of <u>life</u> is the need to replenish the species.

Other laws of physics and laws of nature are more subtle but every bit as real as gravity and must be obeyed. Individuals or species that fail to obey these laws eventually are eliminated from the gene pool."

Natural law, in religion and philosophy is a system of right or justice held to be common among humans, derived from the natural world rather than society. That was the case when Paine wrote *Common Sense*. The problem is that what we historically referred to as natural law evolves as we learn more. (For example, American common law in the 1600's taught that there was a hierarchy of races; topped by Whites with Blacks and Indians at the bottom.) Thomas Aquinas in the 1200's defined natural law as the preservation of one's own good, the fulfillment of those inclinations which nature taught to all animals and the pursuit of knowledge of God."

Here we are speaking of something different. To us, natural laws are not based on beliefs, but on empirical facts, actual laws that govern nature. Most philosophers believe that there are two distinct types of truth. One is based purely on fact and is derived from observation of nature where virtually every observation is in agreement and there is little or no variance. An observer today would see the exact same thing as an observer a thousand years ago or a thousand years into the future. A fact is hard data and no matter how you look at it, it is always the same. Evolution is now an accepted natural law, with natural selection a critical part of how evolution works.

The other type of truth is one based on opinion. Opinions are not truth, but this truth is based on opinions. Both are different from facts. This definition of truth is what one believes after looking at facts. But the facts considered are not the same from person to person and often even the same facts are interpreted differently. Non empirical facts may change. For example, one can state a truth such as I am in Denver and at that moment it is truth. But two hours later by jet, it may not be the truth. Much of today's media is tainted by the writer's opinions. (Many now have replaced the term Natural Rights with Human Rights. But the problem with historical revision and opinion remains.) To keep things clear in this writing, we will use the term Truth to mean what people believe based on their experiences and opinions and Natural Law to mean hard factual observation.

Next, let me discuss Dave's ideas on a human's battle for territory and time, and why honor among participants is critical.

"Humans like other species battle for territory, again this is equivalent to wealth. Humans have the capacity to understand that they are individuals, that they own themselves. Since they own themselves, they own their own time. Since they own their own time, they own the wealth that they produce or acquire with their time.

If a dead guy could answer the question, 'what is the most valuable possession,' he might answer, time. You can't take your possessions with you into the afterlife, so the only thing we own of permanence is time here on earth. When someone steals your possessions, they are stealing your time, a piece of your life.

The greatest goal of humans is to reproduce more of themselves. Some, for personal or societal reasons, choose to support the reproductive goals of others rather than reproduce themselves. To reproduce they need territory (wealth). The instinct to gain wealth is not something that can be turned off in some people. For those who are really good at it, and driven, they can produce a lot of wealth. For those people the drive continues, but the motivation becomes more like a game where they challenge their current selves to outperform their former selves. Some people will gain enormous wealth through one idea or effort that mushrooms way beyond their original goals.

For most, gaining wealth with as little effort as possible requires a degree of control over other people. For four thousand years that control was often absolute. Slavery simply meant that for some they didn't own themselves. They were bought and sold, families broken up, subject to any abuse without hope of redress. (The list of abuses during slavery would take another book, but remember, the only thing that made slaves valuable was the time they worked to create wealth for their owners.) Their time was owned by others who directed their lives and stole their time. In the current era, control in America is generally conducted through a mutual contract between an employer and employee. The employee voluntarily provides some of their time in exchange for some amount of benefit, currency, wealth.

Humans have the ability to enter into contracts with each other. Collectively we create laws, which are simply human contracts. 'Don't steal my time and I won't steal yours.' For contracts to work, the people involved need to be honorable, they need to make good on their commitments. Sometimes similar people will gather to collectively negotiate their situation.

The employer pays the employee to help create goods or services, then sells those to the public (customers) who voluntarily offer some of their wealth to pay for them. If you think about it all three transactions involve offering one's time for some benefit. The modern capitalist system relies on honorable participants doing what they contract to do. In a well-functioning system, the honor among the participants is as constant as gravity, approaching a natural law. When the participants cannot rely on each other to fulfill their responsibility the system breaks down.

Unfortunately, the need to gain territory with as little effort as possible remains constant. Even less than honorable humans are driven by it and use their intellect to deceive their fellow man rather than enter into mutually satisfactory contracts. In nature deception has occurred for thousands of years. For example, the Cuckoo bird will lay its eggs in the nests of other birds and deceive those birds into raising its chicks. This is a classic example of using deceit to gain territory for their offspring with the least amount of effort.

Among humans who honor the system, the rewards may not always be equal, but they are always shared faithfully consistent with the agreement. The distribution depends on where an individual's contribution fits with others involved. Some humans who deceive the system simply take from others with no effort to provide benefits to the other parties. In every ecosystem there are similar species, who's existence depends on other individuals with no thought of mutual benefits. For example, there are wasps who lay their eggs inside other insects who's offspring then eat their host from the inside out. Mosquitos suck in the blood of mammals in order to nourish their offspring. In the animal world we refer to these creatures as parasites. In order to explain away the breakdown among humans, many humans, especially if they empathize with those breaking their contract, justify the behavior by stating new truths. 'They never had a chance, so we can explain away their bad behavior.' (Remember, Truth is based on an opinion of select facts, and the person stating that new truth may really believe it. But others, looking at a different set of facts or the same facts in a different light may disagree.)

Among humans, deceit is used by those who are unprepared or bad at producing goods and services that consumers want to pay for. Or they don't recognize that those who are legitimately creating wealth are investing their time and doing their part. Many feel that those with wealth are not entitled to what they have. Perhaps those using deception do not feel they have the skills to succeed. Or they may just be lazy. For whatever reason, they use deceit to accomplish their personal goal of gaining as much wealth as possible with as little effort as possible. But in this case, they are upsetting a balanced system where other humans are honoring their agreements with one another.

This does not mean that certain individuals, because of physical or emotional problems, cannot be full participants in the economic system. Part of the honorable participation is to help those who cannot help themselves. In the United States the citizens have always extended a hand. They offer their time and a share of wealth to others. But many in this country do not understand the capitalist system. They see it as unfair. They call on government to institute more equity. Life is not fair. Nature is not fair. Inequality and the need to improve one's position is the fuel that drives innovation and constant expansion of opportunity for all.

Humans are unique in that they have developed non-conflict practices to compete. While some government intervention is necessary, such as anti-trust laws, most government intervention, with the best of intentions, only perpetuates the inequity and punishes those who are honorable participants in the system. Compounding the problem is that the non-conflict practices created by man, including laws, are not embraced by all. How can this happen? The vast majority of America's citizens have little or no knowledge of civics (how society and government interact) or of how the capitalist system works in our Constitutional Republic."

Standing firm on truths that do not create opportunity, often widely accepted truths, is pure folly and just throws up roadblocks to progress. Ralph Waldo Emerson believed that nature is intelligible, is law governed and structured in accordance with rational principles. Natural law may be part of one's truth, but simply believing that truth does not mean that it is a natural law. Natural law tells us that men and women of normal physical and mental ability all have the ability to create wealth for themselves and their families. It tells us that they will seek ways to do that with as little effort as possible. It tells us that humans will seek others to help them succeed and in turn will be part of others succeeding. Natural law also teaches us that those relationships are based on contracts between the parties and also laws which are simply agreements that govern relationships. Those who do not honorably live up to those contracts damage and bog down the economic system, or worse, hurt their fellow citizens.

Here is Dave's treatise on America.

"Americans today are perched on the very top step of the wealthiest, most successful society in world history. They have no idea how they got there, and often are being taught to tear it down. The creation of this nation is rooted in one word, LIBERTY.

Liberty, individual freedom can only be in proportion to individual responsibility. In America, we own ourselves and we own what we produce. (The bible speaks to this for those who believe in it. Second Thessalonians offers, "if man does not work, he shall not eat.")

With great freedom comes great responsibility. Wealth is only created through human effort. The most basic building blocks of wealth, food clothing and shelter are clear examples. If you go sit on a rock and do nothing you create no food, no clothing, no shelter. You fail the system, but in today's world much of the time someone will come by and offer you some of their wealth to feed you. Nobody has a natural law right to order them to help, but they usually will. Up until the introduction of government welfare, those who sat on that rock usually felt thankful for the help and committed to doing their best to pay it back. What changed? Today many believe that the help is provided by government, but government on its own creates no products, no wealth. It merely takes from some to give to others.

Everything you use that has been created by humans was made through human effort. There should be no free lunch. When you enjoy something created by humans without trading your own produce, in a way you are either stealing from society or at least mooching. If the benefit came through a voluntary social benefit organization, you should consider it a loan with a plan to give back. If it came from government, then government took someone else's time and wealth. Often the politicians who took it will now appeal to you to vote for them as your benefactor. But between the real benefactor, a taxpayer and you, government will waste a huge amount of what they collected.

Why is government so inept at using wealth (capital), and at producing goods and services efficiently? **There is no feedback loop.** *There are no consequences for inefficiency. To remove the feedback loop eliminating the consequences of incompetence also eliminates the function of the natural law of natural selection. The quicker an individual or organization feels the consequences of inept behavior, the quicker they can make a course change. For too many politicians an alternate feedback loop is working. Citizens offer, 'You don't really give me enough, but if you promise to give me more, I will vote for you.' Why would you encourage a government that simply cuts up the pie into smaller* *and smaller pieces instead of one that encourages you to put your time, creativity, innovative skills to work to make a bigger pie?*

The American experiment depends on a social contract between its citizens. America's citizens own themselves. They own their time. They own the products of their efforts. Every human from the stone age has relied on accurate perception of reality to make decisions, to assure their success. An accurate perception followed by wise decisions within a system that encourages success, not just survival, is the single greatest asset an individual can possess. The free thinking afforded to America is why it leads the world and is the envy of peoples across nations. (There are three nations in the western hemisphere that do not believe in this principle, in rewarding people to make the pie bigger. Venezuela, Cuba, and Nicaragua promote cutting the existing pie into smaller and smaller pieces and all are hemorrhaging educated and skilled people.)

Americans created a government whose greatest function is to protect those freedoms. Among the citizens, physical and behavioral variations will lead to different outcomes, but most critically, each has the right to go as far, accomplish as much, and enrich themselves as much as possible."

Emerson writes, "Every rational creature has all nature for his dowry and estate. It is his, if he will. He may divest himself of it; he may creep into a corner, and abdicate his kingdom, as most men do, but he is entitled to the world by his constitution. In proportion to the energy of his thought and will, he takes the world into himself."

In another writing, Emerson's method became clear. "Some play at chess, some at cards, some at the Stock Exchange. I prefer to play Cause and Effect."

Emerson's discussion of man in the natural world is sometimes portrayed as a simple discussion of environmental issues. Nonsense, he was among the first to clearly call out man's role in the environment. He felt that man separating himself from natural laws, "essences unchanged by man," would lead to man losing touch with the rules of his creation. He would miss out on the teachings of the natural world.

DAVE'S COMMENTS ON NATURAL AMERICAN PEOPLE

"America is the melting pot of the most aggressive, self-reliant, freedom loving people on earth. Their DNA is hardwired into natural Americans. The environment created by our Constitutional Republic has allowed the human spirit to soar. Instead of criticizing the perpetual engine of self-interest, we need to embrace people making a better life for themselves and their families, it is a natural law like gravity. The American free enterprise system is one where people prosper by living up to their contracts with other people; by pleasing others with their innovation and inventions, products, and services. The more they please others, the more they prosper."

The human mind is the pinnacle of God's creation. It is not government, and certainly not well-meaning white people who believe that those with darker skin cannot succeed without their help. What rubbish. All too often those white people are the children of wealthy parents; kids of parents who didn't start them at the bottom of the family company. Kids who see entry level work as beneath themselves and therefore below anyone they might want to help. Again, what rubbish. Many of these people fit into one of two categories.

Some have lived lives of leisure, spending endless years in school, without ever creating anything themselves. As Mom and Dad have given them the means to do little for themselves, they believe that government should do the same for others. The second group that seems to drive this behavior are people in academia. Over and over while in school, I heard professors complain that they weren't running things since they were the only ones who had devoted years of their life to study. It infuriated them that businesspeople and people in sports and entertainment earned more than they did. After all, the academics were the people who had devoted their lives to research and study of society and its ills. To both of these groups you could not tax the populace enough to put money into their careers and research. These two groups drive the political rhetoric that the system is unfair and those who built wealth don't deserve it, it's okay to tax it away. This rhetoric and the policies derived from it have done little to help society. They have become little but devious devices to transfer wealth, not build wealth. This rhetoric divides us.

Just so you don't think I am painting all people from academia with the same brush, I acknowledge the diversity of thought that somehow is hanging on in America's schools. Many who teach traditional views of history, the economy, success, and cultural interaction offer a valuable counterweight. But watch what happens when they try to bring conservative speakers on campus. Today, even tenured professors can be fired if a large portion of their students find their classes too hard; classes that have been taught the same way for decades. It's now unfair.

I love this example from Dave. "Imagine an Easter egg hunt with a bunch of kids. The supply of eggs, like human imagination is unlimited. Generally, the older kids will be more adept at finding eggs than the young ones. A portion of the kids will be highly motivated and more exceptional at finding eggs than others. (Many of the successful egg finders will re-hide some of their eggs for the smaller kids.) Rather than employing their imagination, alertness, concentration, and hustle, some of the hunters will resort to simply following the successful hunters, picking up only what is missed. Their motivation for wealth, eggs, will turn to envy and their motivation will shift from finding eggs to acquiring some of those already found. The unmotivated children missed the instructions that pointed out that there was an unlimited supply of eggs. To them, like in the economy, they see the pie as finite with the slices cut smaller and smaller as more want a piece."

The American Constitution requires government to bow to the individual instead of the individual bowing to the government. Anything that limits or impairs the individuals drive to succeed is damaging. The Natural American is his own king, policeman, and his own beneficiary. With his freedom and unlimited access to his faith and beliefs he is his own priest, or rabbi or mullah. He Is free to create his own wealth, whatever that is to the individual. He is free to share it. Unleashed, with limited government intervention the Natural American is a dynamo of productivity and creativity.

In a conversation with one of my most liberal friends I was chastised for discussing the Constitution in a conversation about civil rights. My friend offered that he defends minority rights. I countered that individual rights are paramount. But minority rights are more important, he said. The conversation ended with my observation that there is no smaller minority than an individual. If you can protect the rights of each individual, it becomes almost automatic to protect the rights of groups and the society as a whole. But only if each of us, as individuals, do no harm to fellow citizens and protect their right to succeed.

Natural Americans are their own kings and queens. They own themselves. **You own yourself.**

In summary, a Natural American believes:

1. That they are born with ownership of themselves and because they own themselves, they own their time.

2. Because they own themselves, they have the right to pursue life, liberty, happiness, and property for themselves while respecting the same rights for others.
3. Forces of greed will never quit. The desire to gain as much property with as little effort as possible will always be with us.
4. Self-ownership, accepting natural laws, Judeo-Christian values in concert with similar values of other world religions are what has made America the greatest country in the world.
5. Honoring the rights of your fellow Americans is a sacred covenant that should never be broken.

In this section, we speak of Natural Americans, but does that include immigrants? First, one of the traits of a Natural American is that they follow the rules, such as immigration laws. But with that said, anyone who wants to come to America legally, to build their wealth legally and who commits not to harm their fellow Americans is a Natural American. Almost inevitably they will go on to extend a hand to others, to help others.

> **"Good people do not need laws to tell them to act responsibly, while bad people will find a way around the laws."**
>
> —Plato

The capitalist system, with its contracts, as practiced by honorable men has fueled a nation of enormous wealth. Poverty as defined in America, experienced by about 13% of American families, corresponds to upper middle class in most of the world. Can we do better, absolutely. How, eliminate programs that led some to doubt their ability to succeed. If the 2021-2022-time frame has shown America anything, it is that there are lots of jobs at every level, jobs that allow Natural Americans to create wealth and together make the pie bigger. Facebook and political blogs are alive today with posts from people who "do not want to be exploited." This misses the whole strength of the capitalist economy. But for those who want to live a life where no others count on them for financial success, the economy offers several opportunities, beginning with creating a business or individual trade skill or artistic talent where you only have to count on yourself. But if you don't want to do any of these things, you will have to enter the economy somewhere. Accepting a job where you work for someone else who needs to make a profit is not remotely like slavery. It is not 'being exploited.'

> "Some people see private enterprise as a predatory tiger to be shot. Others look at it as a cow they can milk. Not enough people see it as a healthy horse pulling a sturdy wagon."
>
> –Winston Churchill

The strongest model for the United States is the one that got us this far. We should be, and in most cases, still are a team of motivated individuals pulling the sturdy wagon. We are a nation that should be encouraging every person to help pull the wagon. We should be constantly making the pie larger. The concept that someone is held back from succeeding, that the barriers to full participation bar success is the antithesis of what drives a Natural American. Every one of us faces barriers, some admittedly larger and more challenging than others. But any narrative that encourages any American to dwell on the obstacle instead of how to get over the obstacle is only keeping that person from using the system to succeed. And as one in a family succeeds, or one in a tribe or community they show others how it is done and often create the exact opportunities that those where they came from need. Ultimately, the only tribe that matters is the American tribe.

Let us take a moment here to discuss K-12 educational opportunity. The current American educational system is made up of parents personally educating their children, traditional public education, charter schools, private and prep schools, on-line and self-learning opportunities, and religious schools. The overall performance of traditional public schools has been falling since President Carter created the Federal Department of Education, four decades ago. The majority of educators know something needs to change. Pay for great teachers is woefully inadequate. Pay for good teachers needs to be improved. Poor teachers are already overpaid. Pay and performance should perhaps be linked. That is if the obstacle to teacher success is removed. But pay is just one part of the puzzle.

I am not going to get down in the weeds on this issue but believe that the idea of a teacher faced with a classroom of kids from broadly diverse backgrounds, languages, and preparation in the name of equity does a disservice to the most prepared, those in the middle and those who need more help. In a classroom of thirty how can any teacher provide what such a diverse group really needs. (The goal should be to provide each student who owns themselves with the best opportunity. Many schools speak to this individual lesson planning and then ask their overburdened teachers to manage to that without adequate time.) Among the worst performing school systems in America are ones where the teachers are paid well, and the schools are funded. Ask, why was it that the majority of religious schools remained open during the pandemic and why their graduates consistently succeed. How would it help those students or any others if we slow them down?

Melody, and her friends are probably the best to rethink how the education system might be restructured. Afterall, those of us on the other side are uneducated Neanderthals. What we would hope you come up with would not be a one size fits all approach, but one that helps everyone advance at a pace that allows them to reach their potential. It would be one where parents are in control, working closely with teachers and where children of parents who do not want or cannot exercise control get help. It would not be critical of religious or private education but would emphasize what they do best. This is the one area where we fully agree with you in that there is a severe systematic problem in our society. There are some great public schools in America, but there are also some who have settled for pumping kids in one end of a pipe and out the other, hoping something sticks along the way. The A, B, C, D, F, grading system has become the A, B system because it makes those who are failing uncomfortable and harms the school's image and funding. Pre-K education may help, especially for kids from households that do not or cannot offer quality education preparation. But for those kids who are prepared, why waste the money? Why bore prepared kids with lessons they already have mastered?

The social concerns that divide many in education need to be secondary to education in the traditional subjects, and both parents and teachers must agree on the content. Again, the laws of unintended consequences need to be considered. For example, one district in Colorado initiated a blanket policy of parents in control but the policy adopted was so broad that school nurses couldn't put a band aid on a scratched knee. A little common sense here.

What is clear is that parents are deciding that they own themselves, and they own the responsibility for their children and the 100-year-old model for America's public schools is not one they have confidence in. It is only a matter of time until they put their pocketbooks where their heart is. The concept of advancement guided by age is obsolete. Advancement for students and faculty must be guided by performance. The transition might be tough, after all we have become so sensitized to how others feel that we really struggle to hurt their feelings, even if that is what is needed to help them succeed. (Later, you will read about how failure was a critical part of how the wealthy became wealthy.)

In the late 1950's I attended an elementary school with children of migrant families who worked in the agricultural fields. One remarkable thing became obvious. Children of these families who moved regularly seldom had an opportunity to complete more than a few months of school in any one place. But the education they received was treasured. Watching a twelve-year-old boy engaging with eight-year-old kids in the third grade classroom was an eye opener for me. They knew they were different, and at a different level. Most twelve-year-old kids were in the seventh grade. But they were hungry to learn and took school seriously. Unfortunately, you seldom see this anymore. It is almost impossible because of the legal concerns and challenges to put protections in place. If a twelve-year-old kid is only at a third-grade level, we need to accommodate them, perhaps in remedial classes and quit stigmatizing them or pressing them into classes where they grow frustrated and quit.

Okay, you now know that this old grey-haired man honors and respects what he refers to as Natural Americans. You also have a clear perspective of what Melody believes. Why is this important? Simply put, reconciling our differences, or at least understanding each other is the only way to bridge the left-right, liberal-conservative divide in our nation, a gaping wound in society.

Where Melody sees things like inequity as a major problem in America, I see it as a critical driving factor in success. But I believe that we share similar goals and are looking for similar outcomes. So, how do we get there? First, we need to take a clear look at the differences.

"The surest way to corrupt a youth is to instruct him to hold in higher esteem those who think alike than those who think differently."

—Frederick Nietzsche

3

HOW MELODY'S VIEWS AND OURS DIFFER

*How Melody's truth and those of the
Natural American differ*

FIRST AND FOREMOST, we differ on the concept of equality and what that means to people. By definition, equality means equal or of the same size or importance. Melody, you believe that because the economic pie is not cut or distributed in equal portions, that it is unfair. I agree. But I would argue that the fact our society and economy allow for and even encourages different outcomes is one of the engines that has fueled America's success. It isn't supposed to be fair, and overall, that is good for America. You indicated that the vast majority of the time, you believe that equality comes before freedom. I would offer that you probably would not give up freedom for equality.

You offered a description of America as beautiful, diverse, immature, and confused. You spoke to your feelings that some individuals have more rights than others. Your summary indicated that you felt that America was not any more special than every other country. Here again I can agree that beautiful, diverse, immature, and confused is an apt description. Without speaking to the physical beauty of the nation, I believe that the people make the nation beautiful, and like the physical diversity, much of its strength comes from it being the most racially and culturally diverse nation on earth. I believe that America matures a bit more every year and fully agree that right now we are a bit confused. Our beliefs are being tested.

One of the places that we are confused is on the subject of the rights of the nation's citizens. Unlike almost any other country in the world, Americans have a written list of rights set down in the Constitution and the Amendments that make up the Bill of Rights. They are explicit and are never to be ignored or unprotected. Ask most British citizens and they will tell you one of the things they are most envious of is **America's Bill of Rights. They have nothing like that.** So why do some Americans perceive that some have more rights? Is it because some have different outcomes than others? Is it because some have better outcomes than others?

From the end of Civil War reconstruction to the 1960's, a period of 90 years, much of society ignored the rights of some citizens. Beginning in the mid 1960's we overcompensated by asking government to carve out special rights for some. Then we struggled to deal with the conflicts created as government set out different rules for different groups. You made it clear that you believe that responsibility comes before privileges, and I agree. But you seem a bit confused at which is more important, rights, or obligations. I believe that they are one and the same thing. The rights of all depend on all fulfilling their obligations. We all have the obligation to honor other citizens' rights, but we can't succeed for them.

Your thoughts on capitalism and wealth are right on the money in that money has become the god of capitalists. On a purely economic basis, the purpose of capitalism is the expansion of the economy to reap the benefits derived from capitalism, from food, clothing, and shelter to all of the additions offered in a wildly successful economy. Those that understand and exploit capitalism well, do it to create wealth, capital for themselves and their families. You go on to note that "our job is to help each other, not profit off from each other. Here I differ. I believe that the Free-Market Capitalist system has proven to be unsurpassed for allowing the individual to prosper, and also has allowed the formation of capital beyond that needed to support a simple living. This excess capital fuels the extras in life like art and music and literature as well as sports and entertainment. It is also what is available to offer a helping hand. Here, at the risk of using an old cliché, we mean hand up not hand out. The entire system depends on the individual succeeding in an interdependent system where people, at any given moment, are on different steps of the financial success ladder. Each person on that ladder is both exploiting and helping both those above and those below. That success ladder is the foundation of financial prosperity.

You seem to think that inherited wealth is by definition bad. One alternative is that you liquidate privately owned companies, and the government takes all the funds. Or government takes over the companies and runs them into the ground as they are terrible at management. Or perhaps the farm that has been in the family for generations goes to… whom? Or the mother or father dies young, with only the estate available to take care of the survivors, but there is no estate, because inherited wealth is bad. Among the most successful organizations in the world are those handed down through the generations. The capital reinvested in American society by trusts and non-profits funded by the wealthy endowing their money in causes they support, is now greater than the total capitalization of the majority of the world's economies. Think about that, money from wealthy people doing good work in America now exceeds the entire economy of most of the nations on earth.

Your comments on both social justice and financial justice seems focused on equal distribution of wealth. Here I disagree with you in that the very essence of equal distribution of the pie creates huge <u>disincentives</u> for making the pie bigger. But with that said, I agree with most of your discussion. Removing barriers to an individual's opportunities, and fairness in education are critical. Where we disagree is your assumption that most of these barriers are historic and systematic. They are not, nor are they fixed in our Constitutional Democratic Republic. Rather, most of them are the dregs of creating social legislation over time that tries to get around the limitations of our founding documents. We have created an avalanche of regulations that are intended to take what one or another group believes needs to be changed (<u>at any one moment in time.</u>) The results of many of these regulations has been to limit or discourage people from achievement **opportunities** guaranteed by the Constitution.

To expand on another one of your observations, the majority of time you feel both social and economic justice is better than 50 years ago. I agree with that and will offer some ideas on just how much progress has been made, and how it came about. It can be better.

Your answers on how to help the national and your personal economic success seem to indicate that you really struggled to find an answer. First, helping the national and your personal economic situation should really focus on saving money, not spending it. You pay your taxes, but have you ever considered what you would personally rather fund with your hard-earned dollars? Do you really believe that government is using your dollars where you would like to see them spent? It is troubling that, outside of college course work, the education of our citizens on the strengths and weaknesses of capitalism and socialism has been relegated to social media. This is especially true when a clear discussion of the differences could be done in an hour. We will tackle a very brief overview here and encourage more personal research. After all, this is the foundation of your personal, your city's, your state's, and your nation's economic well-being. Everyone would like a little more, including teachers, public servants, waitresses, salespeople, mechanics, and entrepreneurs, but where does the money come from? We should have an open a conversation on that.

Throughout these discussions, we will address another of your concerns. You note in your comments that many of our institutions including the Constitution itself is outdated; that the world has passed them by. You seek some revision or reinterpretation of the founding documents. You feel that the socio-economic structures and institutions do not address the problems faced by people in this country today. Inherent in those feelings, is the perception that mankind or citizens today struggle with different problems than in the past. In fact, the whole WOKE movement is based on the population finally awakening to problems that were ignored in the past. Why hasn't America's success included remedying social issues? Look at the historical discussions that follow and judge for yourself whether two hundred years of American history is too long to find solutions.

Without shortcutting the contents that follow, let us close this chapter with an **observation of the Roman statesman and philosopher, Marcus Tullius Cicero.**

- "Six mistakes mankind keeps making century after century:
- **Believing that personal gain is made by crushing others;**
- **Worrying about things that cannot be changed or corrected;**
- **Insisting a thing is impossible because we cannot accomplish it;**
- **Refusing to set aside trivial preferences;**
- **Neglecting development and refinement of the mind;**
- **Attempting to compel others to believe and live as we do.**"

Cicero died on December 7, 43BC, more than 2,000 years ago and he was speaking of the preceding centuries. It is amazing how little man has changed yet each generation seeks to see itself as more enlightened.

Melody, I won't offer any pressure or incentive for you to change your mind. I will simply offer some comparisons and alternative ways of looking at the American experiment. Unlike societies where the culture and economic system is set in stone, ours is always changing, always evolving. If all we accomplish is to tone down the rhetoric by documenting that those who see different truths than you or me are not by and large, selfish, racist, uncaring, brutes, we will have made progress. At the same time, I hope to offer a bit of perspective on the nation's founding, its founding documents, its economic system, and the institutions that are derived from that. Before we radically rework the founding documents and institutions or throw them out, let's take a look at how to make them work for all of us. And by that, I mean all. Now on to the economy.

EIGHT RULES TO LIVE BY

Be clean both inside and out

Neither look up to the rich nor down to the poor

Lose, if need be, without squealing

Win without bragging

Always be considerate of women,
children, and older people

Be too brave to lie

Be too generous to cheat

Take your share of the world and let others take theirs

—George Washington Carver

4

YOU, ME, AND THE AMERICAN ECONOMY

Our discussion of the American economic system, different truths

THE COMMENTARY ON Real Americans begins with the economic premise, that each of us will naturally try to maximize what we consider wealth with the least possible personal effort. Basic economics? For a lot of us, economics looks a lot like higher math; complicated, difficult to understand and to be avoided. For many, economics are like that really toxic friend of a friend who just happens to be able to fix anything. You don't want to be around them, but sometimes you need their help. You can't avoid either. But if you don't understand how the economy really works, you can't maximize it for yourself or help others.

So, it is with the very simple economic premise explored in this section. **You** are the most critical part of the economy. No complicated economic theory here. You are part of an economy that offers both exquisite experiences and some that are more foul tasting. The important thing is, **NO ONE OWNS YOU.** You can participate in the economy or not. If you want to really succeed, you will have to really work. I don't mean go to work, I mean put a lot of sweat, energy, and time in. You will need to create a map for yourself, because if all you do is sit in one place, doing the same thing, then you will watch those who embrace opportunity run right past you. Should you choose to pigeon-hole yourself, limit yourself, you also limit what you can expect from the economy. How does the American capitalist economy work?

SURVEY COMMENTS: Melody, your comments on economic issues were pointed and reflected strong opinions. The American capitalist system is not equal, it does not produce equal results for its citizens. It absolutely favors those who prepare, are creative and work really hard. There have been roadblocks thrown up that created higher hurdles for some more than others. There are people who are wealthy to the point where they couldn't possibly spend what they have, while others scrape to get by. Every one of these statements is true. It is the solutions to these issues where we would open our discussion. Remember the difference between an argument and a debate; in an argument we are struggling for understanding and not to win. So, what about you, those you worry about, and the American economy?

I would propose that equality is a negative in the economy. Equal distribution of wealth sincerely limits your personal ability to really grow your wealth. Equality will not create opportunity for upward mobility. Fewer than one out of five Americans have studied the economy or even understand where they fit into it. So, let's start there.

JOBS are the most basic component of the economy (the private sector).

To put food on the table, clothes on your back and a roof over your head, there are only three options: (1) you go out and earn the money; (2) you or someone else (government) takes money from your neighbors and gives it to you, or (3) you just take it from someone else.

Forgive me for beginning our discussion on a really basic

level. One other observation I've made over the years is that some people are embarrassed to start where I did, at the bottom; probably through envy, or jealousy, or a feeling that they are not being treated fairly, they think they should start in the middle. Maybe at the top.

Let's begin with the entry level worker in any job. What does he have to sell? **TIME**.

That's it, all that worker brings to trade for wealth (income) is their time. Oh, they use their hands, eyes, legs, brain, and other tools, but when you combine them all, you still only have one minute or one hour to sell. You can't cheat the **Natural Law of time**; you can't manufacture more of it. Even in the simplest jobs, we often are not initially good at what we do. The critical thing is that does not need to be a long-term situation.

Here is the story of how I learned that lesson.

When I was just a kid, I worked at picking strawberries. The job entailed bending over or kneeling between two rows of strawberries on a hot day and carefully combing through each plant for ripe berries, picking them, and putting them in small cups in what they called a flat. You got paid for delivering a full "flat" of berries to a truck that would take them to a processor. I was maybe nine at the time and in good shape, still within twenty minutes my legs cramped and my back ached. It gave me great respect for the people in the fields who made a living doing this work. My single mom was always strapped for cash, so if I wanted much more than food, clothing, and shelter, earning it was up to me.

My first delivery was almost my last as the foreman took one look at my work and offered, "The cups are only 2/3 full and half of the berries in those cups are still too green to process. Just leave that flat on the ground, pick up another and pick berries that we can sell." I could tell by the look on his face, that me continuing my career as a berry picker would probably only continue if my second flat passed muster. (Today some people would call that second chance white privilege just because of my skin, but after every day picking berries my pant knees were worn, my hands were scratched, and I was exhausted just like everyone else in the fields.)

In piece work, like picking berries and being paid only for what you produce one of three things happens. You fail to get very good at the job and you starve; (or change jobs). Or you study how others are doing the job and become more efficient so that you can make some money. The third thing that might happen is that after you pick for a while, you develop some personal skills and techniques that allow you to do the job more efficiently and you make okay money for someone who only has time to sell. The employer cares, but it isn't critical to them, because they aren't paying for your time, just the production from you investing your time.

This changes when you get an entry level wage job, let's say flipping burgers. Now you are paid for each hour you work, regardless of how productive you are. Normally the employer will offer training based on how those who came before you did the job efficiently. Again, you will probably start out less efficient than more experienced workers. The employer is paying you the same as other entry workers, for less production. But unlike the berry picker, the employer has an investment in you, the training time, so they will work with you to become better at the job. If you still are slow or make a lot of mistakes that interrupt the work of others or the satisfaction of the customers, they will probably cut you loose and find another trainee. Your responsibility is to offer performance for the time they are paying for.

To many, this work seems lowly and to someone who has an elevated sense of self-importance, demeaning. Nonsense, this is where most people start and get their initial training and skills. Most senior executives start at the bottom. Smart, business owners start their kids at the most menial jobs. They sweep floors or load trucks. Dave's kids started hauling lumber, driving nails, cleaning up work sites and they started before they reached their teens. My kids started washing dogs and doing the same construction work as Dave's kids. It gave them a foundation an understanding of the business and an appreciation for entry level employees. You've given me no indication that growing rich is important to you but succeeding in your chosen field is. Where do people start as reporters?

One of the best ways to improve your lot at the burger joint is to study what you and others are doing and then come up with a better way to do the job. Not only are you more valuable, but you might help everyone else be better. The business produces more, in the same amount of time, can handle more customers, and probably make a little more money. One thing for sure, you will get noticed. While everyone may get a little more pay because improved efficiency means the employer can afford it, you may end up on the short list for any coming promotion or with a new position based on your idea. Your employer will exploit what you created, and it will probably make your life a bit better, OR MORE. You have just experienced the value of improved productivity, and you earned the increase. No one gave you anything. You put your head into your time.

Remember, most employers are counting on their employees getting better. They know that the most productive employees earn them more. They also know that motivated employees come up with ideas that make the whole operation better.

With that said, here is the other side of the coin. Those ugly, uncaring, mean employers who are paying you to do the same thing every day without improvement and productivity gains are not highly motivated to pay you more. You can rant and rave all you want about your personal pay level, but if you are not helping the organization be better, so that it can pay more, you probably won't make more. Your path to wealth is available, but you chose not to take it. It is amazing, for example, how many highly paid restauranteurs of extremely famous restaurants began in fast food.

They were the innovators, the best employees. They learned on the job and improved their wealth opportunity.

But, but, but, you say, the restaurant is only a block from the stadium and the local baseball team is having a hell of a season and people are lined up for burgers for every home game. This place must be making a killing. You're new and weren't there for the last three seasons when the team smelled like old sweat socks, and nobody came to the game. The owner may have taken no wages just to keep the place open. They may have been or are still working 60-hour weeks. The owner may not be very happy to pay people who are not busting it as they dig out.

(In the economic meltdown of the mid 1980's I personally went 22 months without a paycheck, and often personally borrowed the money for payroll, to keep a company together. I didn't lay anyone off but didn't hire replacements for those who left either. The company came out of that stronger than any of our local competitors and boomed the next couple of years. It took three years to get back to where we were before the downturn.)

Progressive thinkers believe that pay and effort aren't necessarily linked. They either do not understand how business works or have an extremely misguided understanding of who makes what. In a 2021 survey of students at the Wharton School (University of Pennsylvania), one of the most prestigious business schools in the world, the majority believed that the average American wage was over $100,000 per year. In reality, the average American wage in 2020, according to the Social Security Administration, was $53,383 and the median wage was $34,612. Among businesses with the lowest profit margins is the restaurant industry as a whole. When pushed to increase pay without productivity and profit improvement the industry's solution is not positive for workers.

An example was the push in the Seattle area a few years ago to increase the minimum wage by 60%. The measure was on the ballot and passed in the region around Seattle-Tacoma International Airport. Restaurants in the area pushed wages to the higher level and at the same time automated order-entry and other functions. The result was that 20% of the employees who might have gotten higher pay, instead lost their jobs. Those that saw the job as an opportunity to get training and grow their skills (getting paid for it), were out of a job. It is easy to be discouraged when you lose an entry level job…where else do you start?

Being out of work is difficult for anyone but losing a job for an entry level worker can be devastating. So will government intervention, for example the push for $15 per hour minimum wage help Americans? Based on the history of continual government ineffectiveness and outright failure, the question is debatable. But even the Congressional Budget Office acknowledges that a minimum wage increases to $15 will help only 17 million workers while it puts 1.4 million out of work. Maybe this is good, but certainly not for those who lose their employment. You need to start somewhere and within reason, it doesn't really matter what the pay is. What is important is for people to participate in the system and then prepare to advance.

The Seattle minimum wage workers who still had jobs were still making less than the median income of $34,612. A full-time employee earning $15 per hour will need a roommate or spouse to live in almost any city in America. If you allow yourself to get stuck at this level, forget wealth accumulation. My point is that employers want people who grow in their jobs and reward them. They want people who prepare to move up, even though they recognize that highly motivated employees may someday outgrow their businesses and move on. This is good. I relish the story of every one of my former employees who grew their success, many of whom went on to become millionaires.

Certain jobs are ENTRY LEVEL and are not really suitable for taking care of a family. The idea that you can pay people $50,000 a year just because they show up, in industries where there is a lot of competition and profit margins are slim is just wishful thinking.

Here's how I learned this lesson.

My grandfather, a farmer, taught me about wishful thinking. I was helping on the farm. I mouthed off about wishing for something and he offered: 'Hold out your open hands, palm up.' Next, he said, 'say wish very slowly.' He cupped one hand in front of my mouth and told me, 'I just caught that word, wish, and I'm putting it in your left hand.' Then he reached down and picked up part of a cow-pie on the ground and put it in my right hand. 'Now tell me which weighs the most, the wish or cow poop.' I think I gasped before he added, 'a wish is only as good as your willingness and ability to make it happen.

The American economic system owes you nothing if you have the ability to produce. It can give you a lot if you use your head, your creativity, and your experience to enhance the value of the hours you sell.

Mark Twain used to put it this way, "Don't go around saying the world owes you a living. The world owes you nothing. It was here first."

Here are some thoughts on making a job a success. ENGAGE, The employee engagement blog lists eight habits of successful employees.

- They are respectful
- They take initiative
- They are professional
- Successful employees are selfless and authentic
- They have a desire to improve
- They take responsibility
- Successful employees stay positive
- They know when to say no and ask for help

There are dozens of sources for similar advice, all relating the same message. The bottom line is that those employees who remain entry level, who do not improve or help the organization be more productive, will probably stay at the lowest end of the pay scale since they are only selling their minimum, time. They control whether they increase their wealth or not.

(There are people in our society who's physical or emotional state allow them only to become productive workers at an entry level, with only minimal opportunity to develop. Many of these people fill important positions and are happy working at their jobs. They are giving their best. They are productive. They are Natural Americans working to help the society as a whole. With a little creativity from management, they can thrive. The key is to fit skills to needs.

Atlantic Magazine, a few years ago reported on a unit in the Israeli Army. The Visual Intelligence Division, Unit 9900 is made up almost entirely of people on the Autism spectrum. While others get bored studying computer screens or photographs hour after hour, looking for tiny details or changes, these soldier analysts find the job relaxing and important. These decoders use their special skills, an extraordinary capacity for visual thinking and attention to detail to do aerial analysis. Their work saves lives of both other soldiers and civilians in a country that has never known a year of peace. Their unique skills make the military more exact and offers a career path for people who might struggle to find meaningful work.

Some people who call themselves liberal only see Israel as an oppressor state. We're not arguing in support of Israel here, merely pointing out how even those with unique physical or mental characteristics can be really successful. These same people can go on into the economy utilizing the special tools they learned in the Army to create wealth for themselves and for society.

Okay you are on the first step, or perhaps just graduating from high school and your focus is on the next step in what I call the **ladder.** This is a great time to look at higher education to better prepare you for advanced careers. Many see higher education as college, and that might be the right choice for you. Specialized degrees, for example in accounting or nursing are often quick tickets into good paying jobs. Advanced degrees, such as an MBA can open a door for a new employee that those without that degree may work years to attain. Beyond the traditional college path, many other opportunities are open to you.

Military service is a great place to gain basic interpersonal skills and technical skills as well as position yourself for a college experience using the generous military education programs. Specific trade schools in high paying fields can allow even faster paths to higher income jobs. Commercial pilot training can now cost over $90,000. Many people work at other jobs to pay for the training and cover the cost of their living. There are financing programs available. Why would you spend that kind of money for a first job that may only pay $30,000? Because, if you are willing to really learn and grow in the job, your first step from entry level may pay as much as $60,000 and within ten years, major airlines are paying pilots from $150,000 to $275,000 per year. Ah, you say, those require time and a step up. You are right. It's up to you.

That bring us to the next step in the **ladder**. I once had this **ladder** conversation with an entry level sales rep. He remembers his response clearly. "What if I try to climb too high and fall off?" He was that literal and, after finding his niche, became successful. Fear of failure assures failure if you never try to do better. Again, the surest way to fail is to not try.

Two thoughts. First, for most of us failure teaches us more than success because we internalize it more. Among business leaders who failed before success are Soichiro Honda, Milton Hershey, Elon Musk, Colonel Sanders, Henry Ford, and Mark Cuban. The list is almost endless, not limited by race or sex. Second, really successful people often find some way to work so hard they succeed even after making a big mistake; they find better ways to do things.

So, the next step is, when you are selling your time use your head to make that time more productive/valuable. Find ways to do things better and implement them. Be better at your job so you stand out and your employer can pay you more. As noted earlier, finding some way to be much better can lead to organizational improvement which opens up new career opportunities. <u>Me Too People,</u> do not get promoted no matter how long they work for a company. Their income growth will be tied to inflation, which means that your increases will be offset by increased cost. If you can be replaced quickly by a new employee, the market value of your time is only as good as your replacement. But an employee who brings innovation to the table may have enormous value as they progress in an organization. Employers do not like to lose creative workers. They often will even support those who screw up if that happens while they are trying to be better.

Develop an idea, even one that requires a great deal of development and help from your organization; it might just be the ticket up. The chapter on Real Americans makes note of what I consider a Law of Nature; that people want to maximize their earnings and wealth with the least amount of effort. If you think about it, what a creative person does when they find a better way to do something fits that model perfectly. They are working to be more productive and taking the initiative. More productivity without killing themselves with effort.

I write this chapter in the month of February, with the television focused on Black History Month. I love this month because we are constantly reminded of Black American success stories. For much of the year, the media spends its time focused on the downtrodden and victims. For some reason they talk mostly of people of color. That focus reinforces a very destructive self-image. If you spend your life having others tell you that other people unfairly put hurdles in your path, it isn't easy to jump over the hurdles you need to clear.

I am not Black, but much of my early life was spent financially stretched, surrounded by field laborers. Even at that age, I could tell which people believed in themselves and which felt they were victims. I watched both racial and economic prejudice as a child and abhor it but met a lot of great people who wiped that stuff off like dust on their jeans. The kids who were raised by parents who refused to let their children feel like victims were the best students in the schools, not the rich kids. I moved thousands of miles away after my mom passed, but I would guarantee many of those kids are now powerhouses in the old community."

Did some of them have different hurdles than me? Yup. Has black America been especially mistreated? Yup. But a hurdle is not a wall, not even a locked door. Why do some believe they are?

In the history portion of this book, we will dig a little deeper into this issue. In the interim, you **own** yourself. You control your own destiny.

Let's discuss the next step in your career path and income ladder: **MANAGEMENT.**

For most of us the first major step up the economic ladder is entry level management, with supervisory responsibilities for people, and processes. Remember the title of manager means nothing to your boss if it doesn't come with you helping the organization be more productive.

(WEALTH, let's consider that wealth means different things to different people.) If your work is to position yourself to devote your time to becoming an artist or writing that great novel, pay for college, or more time with kids, (wealth to you), making more with less effort can open up the time to devote to those pursuits. Innovation infused TIME may completely change your life. Although more likely, your early innovation will just elevate you from worker class to management class. More responsibility, usually more money, and most importantly, this usually comes with more freedom to influence things your way.

One of the most interesting employees that I ever worked with was a man who had a law degree but made his living in sales. To protect his privacy, since I haven't seen him in years and have no idea how to seek permission for this story, I'll call him Tim.

Tim didn't work directly for me. I was an entry level sales manager for a fortune 500 firm after some success as a sales rep. Tim worked for one of my peers. I noticed that he was usually the last one into the office in the morning and was gone every afternoon. At get-togethers, he was the first one to crack a joke or if he'd had a few too many, maybe dance on the bar. You would like Tim.

He seemed focused on what he called his ART, although I never quite understood what that was. He wasn't our top sales rep, but he was always in the top 10%, in spite of what I believed was a less than stellar work ethic.

One afternoon I needed a late lunch, so I walked over to a chain restaurant near the office. There at two in the afternoon sat Tim, an empty beer glass in front of him and two notebooks open on the bar. Curious, I sat down next to him, thinking that a manager finding him in the bar that early might cause him a little discomfort. It didn't.

As I ordered lunch, I noticed that one binder was full of sketches and personal notes and the other extraordinarily organized notes on his job. We didn't have laptops or smart phones then. As we began talking, I noted that Tim had graphs and schedules and copious notes on his job. Tim offered that he tried to get his job done in four hours a day, to leave time for his art and his study. The guy was making a very good living already, and I couldn't help but ask if he thought he might do better with, let's say five or six hours of work.

'Nope, he said. I work better when I stay focused on work, my art, my girlfriend, and my study every day. Eventually I expect to be wealthy enough to do my art full time and I think that I found a girl who will support that. I come here for a beer before transitioning to my art in the afternoon; spend the evening sharing what

I'm working on with my girl, and the mornings studying how to make a lot more money in the four hours I work.

Tim wasn't lazy, but he saw work as simply providing a platform for his ART, his real wealth. What was amazing about the guy was his ability to organize all of the steps in sales, from prospecting for new customers, to developing sales strategy for them, to proposal development, to refining presentations, to closing sales and providing the follow up service to his customers. I had a team of all young people, and I encouraged every one of them to study how Tim worked, and every one of them became more successful.

He only worked for us for a couple of years. He was a Natural American, making his contribution. He made his fellow workers better. To him, wealth was income that allowed time for art, and he achieved both with minimal effort. He was using the company job to pay his bills, and the training to prepare him for the future. (It turns out he was studying for his stockbroker's license, and eventually went on to make a fortune as a broker of penny stocks.)

How does this story apply to you? Let's say you are picking berries and after an exhausting day you say to yourself, "Self, there has to be a better way." Or your flipping burgers and the same thought crosses your mind. You work more creatively and conserve the energy to use your head. Over weeks or months of tinkering <u>on your own time</u> you come up with a tool that makes berry picking much faster. You look at the grill and your spatula and figure out a faster way to grill burgers. Perhaps what you want is to be promoted. You begin studying management or add a business degree. Many corporations now will literally pay you to work for them and support your ongoing education. Your direction through management will depend on your efforts, observation, and preparation. If you can help your team become more productive you all will share in the success.

Generally, managers make more than their employees, but not always. Still management skills can be expanded as you move up the **ladder**. Many complain about how much senior managers make today. Few see themselves moving up into the seven-figure income bracket. Why? In twenty years, you could be the CEO. Most often each step up requires more personal commitment and more creative use of your time. Generally, you will make a higher salary or wage, or...

Boom, you are an entrepreneur, and possibly one who employs others to build your new tool. You still only have so much time, but your earning potential for every hour is greatly improved, potentially because you made something more productive, but also because you are offering the opportunity for others (your employees) to sell you their time. And their time, especially as they become more productive earns **YOUR** business more money.

You **own** yourself. You control your own destiny.

EMPLOYER/ENTREPRENEUR

How do you start a business? You take your idea to make something better, devote time, planning, and energy to that and raise enough money to launch your company. Money, or capital, is the blood of business. That ugly term, capital. You need enough capital to make your business a success, whether it comes from other income, a spouse working to help, family members, a loan or venture capitalists, you need money. Most start-up business fail not because they can't make sales or get contracts, they fail because it costs a lot of money to grow a business. They run out of cash to pay for raw materials, shipping, or staff. Some fail because their business idea or product isn't really needed by the market, but even then, you learn a lot by trying.

But I'm not an inventor, I have no mechanical skills **you say**. No problem, perhaps all you come up with is a better way to organize the work being done. The vast majority of new companies are founded by people leaving one company to start another in a related field because they believe that they have a better way of running an organization. Start at the bottom, learn everything you can and create the life you want. Here's a story that exemplifies this.

A little girl's parents, living in the poorer, primarily Mexican American community of Phoenix, Arizona were keenly aware of the limitations of the local public school. Unwilling to accept mediocrity in the education of their daughter they searched for something better. The woman, a licensed practical nurse and her husband, a veteran and barber, added shifts and a second and then third job to afford tuition in the best college preparatory school in the state.

Upon graduation the daughter defied their dreams and headed to Los Angeles where she learned to play hard, paying for it with a job in the brutal garment industry, a business where discipline is crucial to success. Instead of paying for their daughter's education, her parents continued their own growth, both earning master's degrees in education. One supporting the other, one step at a time, with a disciplined plan. Their dream for their daughter became theirs.

A few years later, the daughter returned to Phoenix and took a job in a furniture dealership, where the Jewish owners recognized her potential, mentoring her and reawakening her educational interests. Within a few months the young woman was taking college classes. In a couple of years, her mentors had helped develop her to the point where she had outgrown their firm.

With a fierce determination she opened her own office furniture store and quickly grew it into a multi-million-dollar firm. She took what she had learned in the garment business about work ethic and the business acumen from the furniture business and moved up the ladder. Her prior employers remained friends and supported her success. She was on her way to creating real wealth and as she added employees, helping others and making her job easier. She had started at the bottom in one of the most difficult industries in the nation, and had grown her knowledge and abilities, courtesy of her first jobs. This is what I mean by Natural American.

(Later, with the death of her mother, her values shifted. She walked away from her business, earned a master's in education, and followed her parents lead, growing children's minds.)

But a little caution here. If you develop the new tool or new way of doing things while on the job, well, your employer is paying you for that. The innovation may well belong to the organization. With that said, many firms will allow employees to patent or copyright ideas with them and compensate the employee. Many employees have become very wealthy taking a share of what their creativity earns, as their employer develops the idea, without the hassle of raising capital or starting or running a business themselves.

And just how much capital will you need? United Parcel Service, the nation's largest parcel delivery service was started by two teenagers with bicycles and $100. Now this happened more than a hundred years ago, so today you would need $3,000 to capitalize at the same level. Almost every one of us can figure out how to raise that much, for a good idea.

For those who look at people who create successful business interests and really improve their family wealth with derision, remember what you see go up can just as easily go down. The case of Wallace Amos is a good example. This Air Force veteran found work with the William Morris Talent Agency but soon plateaued. He parlayed $25,000 of borrowed money into the FAMOUS AMOS COOKIE business which grew from a $300,000 storefront success its first year into a $12,000,000 cookie monster in seven years. He was a darling of talk shows and business publications. But he made the mistake of many entrepreneurs, in that he expanded too fast and then instead of cutting back to what still worked, got caught up in the cycle of bringing in new partners for operating capital. He eventually sold what he had left. This is a common experience, but what a ride, and what a good example. No matter how good your idea is, if you don't pay attention to business basics you will fail. There are literally hundreds of opportunities to learn business basics. In the end, his family wealth was improved, and the lessons learned will always be with him.

Others jump at the chance to prove themselves independent of their prior employer. Often, they will lose everything once or twice before launching their successful firm. Maybe not knowing how you are going to pay rent, or for gas, or for your smart phone, is part of life in a capitalist economy. Capitalists do worship money to some degree because it is the blood that keeps business alive. Think of yourself as similar to an athlete working out so vigorously that your body really hurts. That's what it takes to be a starter on your sports team. You don't notice the pain when you become a star.

Do you have to be incredibly creative or innovative to do better in a job? No, if you go back and look at the habits of successful employees you will realize that an employee developing these traits is valuable to any organization, they need your tools and will pay more for your time. Your path forward is all up to you.

You **Own** yourself.

CAPITALIST

What's next, well you have a little extra money at the end of the month, so you invest it. You expand your company or start a new one. You buy a duplex to rent. More likely you will put it into investments, begin setting a little aside for a rainy day or retirement. Often this set aside goes into the stock market to provide capital to others who are starting their business or expanding one that is already successful. A lot of liberal thinkers don't understand capital. They chastise people with large net worth. But unless the rich put their money in a bag under the bed, every dollar keeps working and helping others. Even that atrocious yacht rich folks buy employees constructor workers and crew. Some think government should just take a bunch of wealth from the really rich. But remember, what we call wealth isn't money, its ownership in a company or real estate, or other investments. Do we really want to force a wealthy investor to sell part or all of a company that they put their life into just to pay more taxes? How will the company perform with new owners? If the firm hits a downturn and there are no capital reserves, what happens to the employees?

"God, how could I ever tell my friends that I have become a capitalist?" This is where it really gets fun. Capitalists put their money to work across the entire society, developing new ideas, making life better for all. Capitalists don't just hand out money. They invest in ideas they believe will be successful, and only those ideas. Don't tell your friends who would be critical. Let your success talk for you. Your future big check to one of your favorite liberal organizations says a lot. Trust me, they won't turn it down.

Over some period, you may find that your investments have grown to the point where they are generating real income from dividends paid by the companies who are using your invested money. Or your wealth comes from carefully studying what companies are doing and buying their stocks while they are not yet successful and selling them when the company values go up. The path to real wealth may be from growing your business, like Bill Gates at Microsoft and Milton Hershey at Hershey, or Elon Musk at Tesla. More wealthy investors are people who study the stock market and invest in successful firms, and then keep on doing that. Of course, these wealthy people run the risk of something out of their control crashing the values of the companies they have money in; losing it all. Since the times when we buried kings and queens with gold around their necks, almost nobody's fortune goes to the grave with them.

What do almost all of these wealthy people have in common? Almost all of them launched their success by working incredibly hard, often 70 or 80 hours a week and by constantly looking for ways to do things better. Some people find that making more money, especially by careful study of the markets becomes their favorite sport and they measure their success in wealth.

What about you? What can you do? Assuming average intelligence and physical ability, you can do just what the wealthiest among us do. But you have to want to and be willing to invest time and effort and eventually money. The American dream is alive and well. The people fighting to come into this country know that, even if many of our own citizens have forgotten it. It astounds me that a high percentage of newly minted billionaires in America are immigrants. If you look around your hometown, I'll bet you find a similar trend among locally successful people. You know the Korean or Mexican family that opened a restaurant twenty years ago and now owns three and the commercial buildings that house them. Immigrants embrace the promise of capitalism, while many naturally born citizens somehow miss the whole point. Many get angry because they envy those with more. Envy is the antithesis of the American dream. Have empathy for those who are struggling, but not sympathy. With empathy you can reach out to help people help themselves. Don't let sympathy turn those with less into victims.

There aren't lines of people clamoring for admittance to Cuba, or Venezuela, in fact their citizens are trying to come here. China has adopted free market, capitalist economics to launch their modernization and meteoric rise.

Why does Capitalism provide more? The primary precept of both communism and socialism is the equitable distribution of production among the population. You take what the economy can produce and share it among the populace. The old Soviet handbook, THE SOCIALIST ECONOMIC SYSTEM, emphasizes, "the constantly rising material and cultural requirements of the whole society, through continuous expansion and perfection of socialist production on the basis of the highest techniques."

You see the problem? Socialism speaks to dividing up production. It fails to emphasize the other parts of what you can do to improve your lot. You can innovate and invent. If a society took 100% of the production of candles and shared them equally, even increased production, that society would still not have electric lights. If that same society emphasized expanding the mining of coal and shared the production, they wouldn't have the improved quality of life from natural gas production and the promise of solar power. (More on coal later.) One person with the incentive to make something better or do it more efficiently, moves society forward. They often become wealthy, improving their life and increasing their family's wealth.

But all that innovation and effort stretches you. Is it reasonable to expect that of yourself?

Gorge Bernard Shaw, the famous playwright and political activist once offered, "The reasonable man adapts himself to the world; the unreasonable one persists in trying to adapt the world to himself. Therefore, all progress depends on the unreasonable man." Make the effort, go change the world; but do it in a way that makes the pie we all share a little better and larger.

Venezuela, twenty years ago, before the Socialist Revolution of Hugo Chavez was the per-capita richest country in Latin America. Chavez was passionate about ending poverty in his rich country. He was a passionate socialist. He held the rich responsible for exploiting the workers, even though the vast majority of workers in the country were middle class. Most of the impoverished were uneducated farmers and laborers. Chavez didn't emphasize education or human development, he focused on how unfair it was for some to be really wealthy.

The country sits on the most accessible oil and gas reserves in the Americas but many of the people, even in the cities, now cook on wood fires in their yards. There is declining gas or electricity for stoves. They cook, if they can find food, using wood but the local trees are disappearing and the forests are being destroyed, usually by educated chemical engineers or out of work oil field workers, cutting wood just to feed their families. The middle class is collapsing, and the poor are desperate. Inflation is thirty times that of the U.S. The rich have either fled or moved what wealth they can out of the country and are living in seclusion. Thousands are trying to cross America's southern border.

What the government of Venezuela did was follow the basic Socialist model. They decided that the government was the best tool to cut up and distribute the huge pie that was their economy at the time. They sliced it into equal parts, except of course for the much larger parts for government officials who would be compensated extra for all the effort; oh, and the armed forces and police who would protect those officials. They collapsed the income of the educated and management class causing a huge brain drain, as their income was slashed; they were also stigmatized for being economic elite. They took what little they still had and fled the country. As industry began to collapse, the pie kept getting smaller. Their oilfields rusted, production dropped, pollution soared. Natural gas fields were shut down because there were no parts to maintain them. Without gas, electricity generation tanked. Prices soared. The government's solution was to nationalize even smaller industries and institutions and use the money taken to subsidize soaring prices for everything. But today, they are wrestling with a simple reality; there is nothing left to take, and the smaller pie won't feed everybody. This is amplified by the lack of innovation and new technology to keep farm production up, and lack of fuel for even the old technology. And there is no money to import foods. The result, equitable misery. Anyone who can do Venezuela research on a computer will discover their own horror stories.

China made the same mistake under Chairman Mao. Cambodia's ten-year experiment led what history calls the killing fields, to the death of millions.

Let's see, create as much wealth as **you** can for your family with the least amount of work. Now let me note one of the problems with this natural law. Without some rules, it can spin out of hand very quickly. If we allow it, the path some will choose in following this natural law will be to stick a gun in your face and take what you have, takers, parasites. That is certainly gaining wealth without a lot of effort. Probably not good for society as a whole, or even for the gunman if someone better armed doesn't want to give up what they have earned. Governments who focus on victims and not producers tend to resemble takers. They take what producers produce in the name of giving it to non-producers. Still in a civilized society with rules and honorable people the natural law holds up.

You **own** you. You control your own destiny.

JOBS IN THE PUBLIC SECTOR

For those of you in drawn to the public sector, I'll divide the messaging into two different groups.

Many are drawn to serve, perhaps in the military or education or medicine. For many, part of the wealth they seek is the public good they can do in these fields. Just like the private sector, rewards come from moving up the ladder, although it might look a little different. A teacher with five years of experience and a master's degree generally earns up to 50% more than a starting teacher. (A first-year teacher may find that they work 80 hours a week since like other entry level workers, they aren't competent in their jobs right away. It may take three or four years to reach a comfortable workload.) Military careers are much the same. Few outside the military realize that most high-ranking officers will have master's or doctoral degrees or even multiple advanced degrees, not in military tactics or doctrine but in international affairs or supply chain management or even psychology. Better preparation makes them more flexible, better problem solvers, and more valuable. They also make a lot more money. Each of these professions requires you to move up the **ladder** for better pay and more responsibility. Most of these careers offer some retirement benefits, but to retire well, use the same tactics as any capitalist, invest a little of your own money each month for your future.

For those who move into government just because you need a job, the path to advancement in responsibility and higher pay is similar. Hard work, targeted preparation for advancement and innovation are the path to the ladder steps. Unfortunately, years of bureaucracy have warped the career paths in many government agencies. In that environment, moving up the steps is often controlled by outdated seniority rules where management is drawn from those with the most years of service. These may not be the best people for the job, but those who have prepared are often excellent. If you are stymied by seniority rules, consider moving to a new agency for advancement. Try the private sector. You own you and you are free to sell your time anywhere.

Are you going to grow very wealthy purely on public sector pay? Probably not. But many of these jobs have really great retirement benefits and after you move up, enough pay to begin a personal investment portfolio of stock or real estate or some other opportunity. Your natural instinct to grow your wealth is still available. You're a Natural American. Senior public service positions often pay comparable pay to upper-level private sector jobs. Across the board, preparation, learning and education, and hard work, opens opportunities. Will you hit a home run like the entrepreneur who builds a successful billion-dollar business? Not likely. They qualify for a bonus for risking everything and pouring their own money into a business knowing they might lose it all. But across the country upper end civil servants live a great life with money and time for whatever they believe is wealth. Many retire young.

DISASTEROUS REGULATATORY PRACTICES

For five decades the American Federal Government has worked to offer the public improved working and living conditions through regulation yielding visible improvements in cleaner air and water and safer working conditions. Anyone who drove the freeways in southern California in the 1970's when the blue exhaust haze blocked out the Santa Monica Mountains, would rejoice in the improvements today. Waterways that were polluted to the point of killing off all of the fish now provide great recreational opportunities. With that said, these same regulatory regimes require a little scrutiny. All too often improvement has come at extreme cost. Any effort to revise regulatory regimes is met with derision. (You don't care about people, you are destroying the environment, you are just a mouthpiece for the oil companies, why are you killing polar bears?) The bureaucrats who administer the programs stifle their own creativity and boorishly adhere to the original ideas and plans even though better strategies become obvious. And once a regulatory agency or set of laws come into being, no matter what the outcome, even total success, they never go away. You see, bureaucracy cannot exist without a problem. (When the Exon Valdez oil tanker went on the rocks in Alaska's Prince William Sound in 1989, a clean-up commission was created to supervise the work. In 2022 with clean-up activities completed decades ago, a version of that commission still exists.)

<u>A bit on the foul-tasting part of the economy.</u> For decades, beginning about 1940, a person with a high-school education could build a really nice middle-income life by working in manufacturing. If they used the income wisely, they could become rich. The continuously improving income came from constant increases in productivity and organized labor making sure that the worker got their piece of that improvement. Trade unions emphasized skill improvement of their members and negotiated wage improvement

from management. Employers were amenable, if not excited about sharing because they knew that experienced workers were the ones that drove productivity gains. Manufacturing technique improvements and worker skills made even old manufacturing plants more productive. They could produce a bigger pie.

At the same time, much of the rural agrarian world began to modernize. Chinese farmers sons became factory workers. Children of piecemeal Indian craftsmen, more educated, moved into automated production. Japanese companies moved into automotive, electronics and consumer goods. Korean shipyards streamlined production of ships. They became competitors.

American factories, pressed hard by Federal, State and Local government for more tax revenues and labor and environmentally sound production, fell behind in modernizing. There is only so much that you can do to a factory designed decades ago. (I'm not excusing corporate management from their part of the blame here.) Production gains stalled. Labor pushed for higher wages without the productivity gains of earlier periods. The squeeze of manufacturers from labor, regulation, changing markets and management's failure to continually focus on modernization made it difficult to rationally modernize factories that were becoming obsolete.

For some reason, under the banner of NO CORPORATE WELFARE, government found it more expedient to offer training to displaced FACTORY workers, (to learn 'new skills'), than to help business modernize production. Why should the public help out all those rich old capitalists who owned the factories? The problem was that many of those 'new skill' jobs had yet to materialize or paid much less than old factory jobs. The second problem is that those old traditional businesses were almost all owned by the millions of stockholders who had invested in them. Much of that investment was from retirement funds. People like you and me balked when management came to us stockholders who were seeing declining dividends and asked for huge additional investments to modernize. Instead, we saw our retirements sink with the old dirty manufacturing firms. The fat cats who could spend all their time watching the market, had diversified their investing, and weren't hurt. You can't blame them for keeping an eye on their investments or taking action. You would too. But your investment was managed by whoever controlled your retirement account.

Many years ago, I was flying into New York, looking for a break from a Navy school I was attending. On approach to the Newark airport, he noticed an ugly smoking mess along a river. The Hackensack River was literally so polluted that it had caught fire. Over the next twenty years the government passed regulations that outlawed the types of pollution that made the river a mess. Not only did they regulate it, but they also passed huge criminal penalties for pollution. So far, so good you say.

The businesses along the river had been old school manufacturing firms. They did dirty jobs like galvanizing sheet metal and anodizing aluminum. They manufactured things from petroleum. They made specialized paint and recycled old equipment. Some turned basic minerals into more valuable products. They had done that work for decades and had well trained, experienced workers. They also disposed of waste into the river as they had for decades. That was how it was done.

Over the next 20 years they all shut down. The river now is much cleaner with nice greenbelts and parks. But the needs those old businesses filled still exist; like treating metals so that they survive the environment better and producing specialized chemicals. Those jobs had paid the employees a really good wage.

The hot dog vendor now serving families visiting the greenbelts makes minimum wage. Those high paying jobs in the old dirty industries are now done overseas, where we have no control over pollution. Many of the families of the dirty job employees have fallen out of the middle class. The wage earners running drill presses, were retrained in service jobs that paid half as much. Many could not find work at all.

Perhaps government could have helped the owners of these businesses who built their firms in the 1940s, many during the war years, modernize into clean production factories. Government had the funds and the ability to help, they had the power to both improve the environment and stabilize these businesses. They didn't, instead turning to the owners and making it clear that it was their problem. But finding that a small factory built for $150,000 in 1946 would cost $1,000,000 to modernize in the mid 1970s was more than the owners could afford. So instead, foreign workers make those products at high pay, dirty the environment, and we send dollars overseas for imported products. Government made feel good efforts to retrain the workers, usually in industries with far lower wages or no jobs at all. Then ignored the real cost of increased welfare and the social costs of despair.

Unfortunately, a lot of those old dirty, manual, high paying jobs used to be filled by non-white workers. As the communities decayed, those willing to relocate did. What was left were stressed communities, often of color, clinging together for mutual support. The tax base collapsed. Social services programs paid people to stay on, rather than move on. Stand up and cheer, the river is clear. The black churches, as in slavery days, offered the people solace and kept the communities together, but they could not change the economics of far fewer blue collar high paying jobs. Some of those churches worked hard to help motivated individual church members move into new solid jobs. Some of the churches, drowning in despair, began looking for a bailout. Families who invested in education had a better chance of seeing their children succeed. Those who believed their kids would follow them into good paying blue-collar jobs often saw different results. Educated kids often moved to where there were better jobs.

The fact is capitalism, by definition, means production and manufacturing in many cases. Government cleaned up the Hackensack River. Perhaps low-income loans might have saved a lot of those jobs, but much of society would rather pay people welfare than help business modernize. The rust belt of America is full of these stories. In some cases, nowadays, 'now there's a word from the 1940's,' Government seems to be learning, but not always.

Our surveys found that most Liberal thinkers support the governments strong environmental push. So, we now make war on coal and coal miners, oil and oil field workers, pipeline companies and operators, logging companies and forest workers, the remaining dirty manufacturing plants and their employees, and the list goes on. These are America's remaining high paying blue-collar jobs. The skyrocketing cost of fuel hurts the lowest income families the most. There doesn't have to be a war on any of these.

In 2005, at the Seattle airport, a middle-aged guy asked if he could join my wife and I at the table where we were devouring some clam chowder. It turns out he was from Yakima and was a former one term liberal Democratic legislator who had somehow been elected from a conservative district. The subject of workers displaced from jobs crushed by environmental regulation came up. "Those companies needed to die," he commented. "Their employees should have been the first to shut them down. If they couldn't see the damage they were causing, they deserve to be out of work." His words ring in my mind like yesterday. Understanding >X, Empathy >X, Family Concerns >X, Foreign Pollution >X; but he was true to himself and his vision of political correctness. And immune to any thoughts of the human costs of that correctness.

Every regulation has consequences. The war on the logging industry has driven up the cost of building homes dramatically. The war on pipelines and oil is, in 2022, driving the highest inflation in four decades. The war on old style manufacturing has created the rust belt of struggling, primarily minority, communities across the East and Midwest. Government's solution has been to pay people to stay and struggle and blame business and successful society for the problem. Why didn't they just build a new factory? None of these things are much of a solution for those left behind.

In the late 1940's and 1950's black migration away from the Jim Crow south provided the manpower to build America's industrial base. To take care of their families, men and women moved to where the jobs were. They did well. But now there is just enough financial support to keep them where they are and alive. Alive is not the American Dream. They are being paid not to be Natural Americans. They are being paid not to participate.

Milton Friedman, the renowned economist, offered a clear picture of governmental social policy. "One of the great mistakes is to judge policies and programs by their intentions rather than their results."

What can you do to help? First do not ever give up your passion for what is right. Second, instead of following the social/mass media on the issues, take a few minutes and research for yourself. Give yourself permission to replace simple slogans with real answers, especially answers that include the blue-collar workers who paved the way for all of us. Get rich and employ anybody you want.

You **own** yourself. Move up the **ladder**, be part of the solution.

"Tell me and I forget, teach me and I remember, involve me and I learn."

–BENJAMIN FRANKLIN

5

DAMAGING THE ECONOMY AND THE CAPITALIST CONTRIBUTION

Socially Damaging Definitions

AMERICAN MEDIA AND many educators have sensationalized problems in this country. Money flows to media that pedals discomfort and unrest. CNN pumped up their ratings by pounding on President Trump. Some criticism was justified, but not four years of an average of five negative stories per day. The Russian connection stories alone seriously damaged any real scrutiny of Russian politics, and it turned out to all be campaign propaganda. The Justice Department spent tens of millions of dollars chasing the Russian story and found nothing. It was all made up and paid for by politicians. OAN and Fox News are masters of exploiting those with conservative views to drive ratings and profits. I personally believe they more accurately portray many stories than CNN, but like CNN they pick and choose what they cover. I noted earlier that the people who pioneered media news must be rolling in their graves.

Grant money flows to universities who trumpet problems. (Even in educational research, once a program gets started, it never goes away, the managers just begin changing the definitions of the problem. (Engine exhaust>global warming->carbon footprint>environmental change>carbon free / voting rights>housing rights>economic inequality>equal justice>ban the police) I'm not making the case that environmental and social issues are not important. I live in Alaska because of crystal clear rivers and wilderness. We are arguably the most diverse state in the Union, not perfect, but with little animosity. The point is that without screaming about these issues, ratings go down and grant money dries up. CNN is desperately looking for a new boogieman after Trump left office as their ratings have fallen 80%.

To simplify the messaging, many have adopted overly simplified arguments. They parrot social media, asking you to accept their societal definitions. Some of us read and listen to both sides and then do our own homework, but not many. "Coal Bad, Solar Panels Good."

Let's start with Coal Bad. Coal replaced wood as a primary energy source in the 1700's. It gives off more heat per ton of fuel than wood, with about the same levels of pollutants. It is easier to harvest and transport. Besides, if the world had continued burning wood, with the growth in population, all of the forests would be gone. As historically used, coal does emit large quantities of emissions, many of which are not good for the environment. The use of coal, especially for power generation has historically been a major source of pollution and greenhouse gasses. But it is cheap and in Alaska alone there is enough coal to fuel most the world's energy needs for a century.

But the media and activists have given coal a reputation as a dirty fuel. In the 1980's with technology to clean up the emissions from coal fired plants still developing, the country and much of the world began to focus on cleaner fuels. A switch from coal to natural gas can reduce Co-2 emissions by more than 50% and reduce carbon dioxide. So, the USA and much of the world began to move toward gas especially for power plants. It was trumpeted by the press as a major solution to coal pollution. At the same time, the use of natural gas for production of chemicals and fertilizer exploded and the use for home heating and cooking expanded rapidly. The price of natural gas has been rapidly rising. Ready reserves of gas are shrinking. Over the next two decades the war on coal expanded to a war on oil and gas. Gas is now a bad thing. The war on fossil energy at just the moment that America became energy independent again has seriously hurt our security both militarily and economically. Alternatives such as solar and wind are much more expensive, so in order to make them attractive the government artificially drives up the energy prices. (Deployment of wind power is actually declining.) The materials used to make solar panels and the manufacturing of them are among the dirtiest refining processes known. Use of rare earths to support virtually all new electronics is exploding, but we cannot get rare-earth mines and refineries open in the USA because the processes are 'too dirty.' We buy them from China where they cover up the environmental costs. The replacement costs of wind generators' short operational life destroy almost all of the economies promised. But because coal, oil, and gas are bad, we spend enormous amounts of money making ourselves feel we are doing something 'good' while seriously hurting those least able to handle the stresses on already strained family budgets. But let's stick with coal here.

There has been a concerted effort to stop all coal mining, and coal use in the country. "Coal is bad." Coal is almost a swear word to many. We should shut it down. At the same time, the ability to clean the emission from coal power plants has improved dramatically, but no one cares, because government is trying to stop coal use and the owners of coal fired plants cannot justify huge investments in making them cleaner. The technology exists to capture emissions and pump them underground where they dissipate over the years, but no one cares. Perhaps even more important, there are technologies to convert coal to natural gas today, even while the coal is still underground, leaving residue trapped in the rock. Filtration systems now exist to strip much of the impurities from that gas, leaving a very clean burning fuel with unlimited supplies of raw materials. Wow, a virtually unlimited fuel source, available in the USA, produced by American workers, that is cleaner and inexpensive. No one cares. Coal is bad.

Did you know these technologies even existed? I doubt it, because it is easier for the media to stick with "Coal is Bad" than explain that maybe that isn't the case. I'm not advocating for coal here but setting the stage for a further discussion of how **damaging definitions used for political reasons** are hurting the economy, business, and you. The challenge is to dig a little deeper, past the sloganeering. Fossil fuels will never reach zero emissions, but we reduced auto emissions by 80% in twenty years, maybe we can do the same across the industry and help out those our policies hurt the most. Without onerous regulation those trying to create more wealth with hard work and innovation could offer alternatives. Many already are, but we aren't listening. Go to work for one of them, invent a real cleansing tool, get rich, save the world.

Am I the only one that is growing concerned as we turn pristine desert environments into fields of ugly silver and black solar panels and the magnificent vistas of our near shore oceans into telephone poles with big windmills on top? Cleaner energy is critical but let's quit letting damaging definitions eliminate alternative solutions. You do not have to parrot the political catch phrases. **YOU OWN YOU.**

Inequality is troublesome, but it has always existed and always will. The war on inequality is unwinnable and since it keeps us from tackling underlying issues, is arguably destructive. If economic growth provides for improved standards of living, better living for all, do you really care if your neighbors can afford a new Mercedes? Is your Chevy any less serviceable? There are 724 billionaires in

America and 20,740,000 millionaires. You probably know several wealthy people. In some industries, the majority are people of color. How many of them are holding you back?

Are you so obsessed with mass transportation that you pay no attention to small towns and rural areas where it is impossible? Many of these same areas are on the outward edge of the power grids where there is not enough excess electrical power to support electric vehicles. Many of these rural communities are close to unused coal fields. Imagine how much cleaner local environments could be if we converted that coal to gas underground to heat, generate electricity and power vehicles. Imagine how emissions in rural areas would drop if hundreds of fuel tankers per week were never on the highways.

"Gas cars are bad." Both the head of Toyota and Tesla have warned that the electrical infrastructure to support even a 50% shift to all electric vehicles will not exist in America for three to four more decades. Each of these companies issue new warnings every few months. Their most recent concerns can be found in a one-minute Google search. Even so, GM, one of those old rust belt companies is milking government support to convert manufacturing to all electric vehicles. One has to wonder whether this, the height of political correctness, is leading to disaster for shareholders and workers. Some communities already limit car charging. Drive your new EF150 pickup up to a remote lake for a weekend of fishing. If it is more than 200 miles from home, you don't have enough power to drive back. Do we really want to extend infrastructure into remote wilderness? What happens if a thousand electric vehicles get stuck on the highway in a blizzard?

I am not arguing that the nation cannot transition to cleaner energy. We all support it but think regulations that limit how we get there are damaging and stifle the Natural American's sense of innovation. To blindly follow the musings of the academic elite assumes they are always right. Remember, it was only 200 years ago that they were arguing that it was okay to enslave black people because they were inferior beings. America's first openly progressive president, former governor and university president actively promoted white supremacy seventy years after the Civil War. He telegraphed the message that black citizens were okay, the country needed them to do menial tasks.

Don't harm the whales. The native people of Alaska, Russia, Japan, and other countries have hunted whales for food, energy, and supplies for eons. Yet animal rights groups pound even these rich native cultures for a critical part of who they are. Whale populations are strong. They were on the edge of extinction when they were hunted for their oil. What saved them? Not government, but the development of the American oil and gas industry, which by the way created enormous wealth for those innovators and the capitalists who 'accidentally' saved the whales.

Save the polar bear. Warming arctic environments threaten the existence of the polar bear. Perhaps, but there is, as of today, twenty years after the media began trumpeting the risk, no decline in polar bear populations. Recent studies show the bears are remarkably adaptive.

Dog racing is bad. Again, animal rights groups are targeting the Iditarod Sled Dog Race as abusive to dogs. Anyone who has ever watched the race has seen the pure excitement and joy the dogs exhibit at doing exactly what they were bred and trained to do. A racing husky mix dog would go stark-raving mad curled up in your lap in an apartment in New York. You do not want to see what a bored sled dog would do to your new REI parka or your favorite book.

RICH PEOPLE BAD

By definition, to many today, it is inexcusable to be wealthy. People with a lot of wealth are pariahs. They couldn't be wealthy without taking money from the less fortunate. But we have just examined how they made that wealth. They created opportunities for others to move up as they made money, they took nothing. Capitalism allows one to grow rich by serving man.

In the earlier pages we tracked the path to increasing wealth. Most of America's wealthy people followed these capitalist steps to grow their wealth. Did their efforts hurt your ability to do the same thing? The answer is no. If anything, they helped put the steps in the **ladder** to your success. If it is natural to try to improve your wealth, to take care of your family, with minimal effort, why do we think of these people as evil? Why do so many look down on capitalism?

The late Walter E. Williams, a renowned economist and professor of economics at George Mason University once commented, "Capitalism is relatively new in human history. Prior to Capitalism, the way people amassed great wealth was by looting and plundering and enslaving their fellow man. Capitalism made it possible to become wealthy by serving your fellow man."

But the programs of the depression hang on today, expanded and championed by millions of Bureaucrats who administer them. Overhead, the cost of administrating any organizations efforts to accomplish something is more than twice as high in government run programs as in privately funded programs. In other words, if government taxes a billionaire a million dollars to support a food program, generally as much as $500,000 or 50% is lost to administration and only $500,000 puts food on the table. If the billionaire gives the same million dollars to a food bank directly more than $800,000 actually goes to food. If he puts the same amount into an education or training program to help people develop skills to advance themselves, the money creates positive results, and the beneficiaries buy the food they want. But don't we need government to tell the wealthy to help, demand it through taxation?

Before the 1940's, in the U.S., churches and local beneficial societies helped the less fortunate. Hospitals raised funds to provide healthcare to those in need. It didn't take 60,000 employees in the Federal Department of Health and Human Services and an additional 100,000 in the 50 State departments to serve the less fortunate. And those receiving aid in the old days were determined to find work and then contribute back to the same groups that gave them a hand up.

During the great depression, economic crises created despair greater than the churches and hospitals could handle. Government stepped in, but that did little to alleviate the displacement of workers. It did give many enough to 'just hold on.' World War II rebuilt the economic engine and launched a spurt in financial growth for the citizens. The modern welfare state does little to help people move up the economic **ladder**. Many scream that government's social welfare programs do not provide a high standard of living. How does the economic pie grow if we pay millions of people not to participate? Social benefit programs should be temporary for all but those who cannot contribute.

Is there any requirement for anyone to volunteer to help to the less fortunate? No, there are no economic or natural laws requiring it. There are religious doctrines and social conscious reasons, but there are no requirements. Yet many wealthy choose to reach out and the liberal media fail to give them credit.

I am reminded of a conversation with the daughter of a wealthy family, small business owner and uber liberal. She and a friend were discussing social investing. After excusing herself for a minute to look up something on her computer she returned to the table with a loud," Damn, damn, damn." It just shocked her to learn that the liberally hated Koch Brothers were among the largest contributors to her passion, Public Broadcasting.

They put their money into programming that they believe is important to what they believe in and because they were true adherents to the concept of Free Speech. If the Koch brothers were not wealthy, they couldn't support Public Broadcasting. If they hadn't focused on the natural law, maximizing their wealth they wouldn't have the money. They know that much of the doctrine of Public Broadcasting does not align with their beliefs, but the concept of making voices heard does.

How about a man whose wealth dwarfed all of his contemporaries? Andrew Carnegie was a businessman and industrialist in the heyday of America's industrial revolution. He was by far the richest man in the nation. His rough and aggressive business practices created a monopoly in steel when it was critical to building world infrastructure. He was feared and hated by many, especially competitors and an enigma to the public.

Before his death, he committed to giving away all of what was at that time the greatest fortune in the world. His wife was committed to help, and they did. They built and endowed thousands of museums and public libraries not only in the USA but across the English-speaking world. Carnegie funded trusts and endowments for the arts, universities, public giving, and world peace. He gave it all away under his moto, "The man who dies thus rich, dies disgraced."

In today's world, he would have been able to accomplish a lot less because those who believe that they have better ideas on how to spend Carnegie's wealth, wealth that they believe he probably didn't really deserve, would have taxed much of it away. Half of what they took would be lost to the bureaucrats.

I personally like the story of a contemporary wealthy family. Leon Cooperman and his wife Toby live in Florida in a five-million-dollar home, much of the cost covered by selling a modest home they'd lived in for decades. They drive old cars, and ride bicycles most places in spite of a multibillion-dollar fortune. Most of the wealth came from helping others grow rich and assisting businesses raise money. Like Carnegie, Cooperman comes from a very humble beginning. Like Carnegie he worked like a dog for much of his life, and even today spends hours a day managing his wealth. I've never met him but would like to.

He watches and manipulates his investments like fly fisherman fish. He works hard to catch fish, and rejoices in a really successful day, and then releases the fish; or in Cooperman's case, gives the money away. One of my passions is fly fishing. Cooperman sees his work like a sport that he dearly loves. He fishes for money. He, like Carnegie believes the key to upward financial mobility, especially to the disadvantaged, is education. And while the Cooperman's contribute to hospitals, food banks, local trusts, and endow programs, their primary focus is on education issues.

They have committed to funding higher education institutions and programs to make it easier for students to afford education to the tune of hundreds of millions of dollars. Cooperman believes that 'the world isn't meant to be totally even.' He is a true believer in the concept of equal opportunity and puts his money in that direction. He and Toby have committed to give away 90% of their wealth to the causes they believe in. That will be literally, billions of dollars. How many depends on how successful the fisherman is in landing new wealth along the way.

Unlike Carnegie, the Cooperman's take a beating from those who do not understand the American economic system, upward mobility, and wealth. A Washington Post article noted some of the nastygrams they receive.

"Billionaires shouldn't even exist in America."

"One day, we're coming after all of you with pitchforks."

"Wake up moron. YOU and your insatiable greed are at the root of our biggest societal problems."

Notable liberal politicians, like Bernie Sanders, AOC, and Elizabeth Warren have criticized this type of wealth.

Leon doesn't get it. Again, according to the Washington Post, he was born poor, went to public schools, borrowed money to go to the university, worked 80 hours a week and lived frugally. He understands the Wealth Gap and is troubled by it and sees the solution as the same as he used to grow wealthy. The capitalist system will allow you to move up.

Others, even those who spend millions on their own yachts, spaceships, and private islands are also plowing huge portions of their fortunes back into society. Many have committed to a binding agreement to give back at least half their wealth before they die. Some are already past that goal. One thing, they understand is the capitalist system and are more capable than some activist or politician. Capable of what? Capable of putting the money where it will make a difference rather than just honor some feel-good slogan or misplaced definition.

I've studied economics, but am not a guru or expert, but to me the three things driving the wealth gap are:

- Firms like Microsoft, Apple and Facebook are sexy and the people who use their products bid up their stock way beyond the actual value based on earnings.

- The stock market has become a well calculated poker game, rather than a tool to fund capital needed to create and grow business and reward those who invest through dividends.

- A lot of people with great potential to build real wealth for themselves and their families don't believe they can, feel they are victims held down by those at the top, or are afraid to try because they won't risk failure.

I'll never be a billionaire, I started modestly. Most businesspeople I know trusted the Natural Laws to guide them into their limited American Dream. My kids will make a better life for themselves and will use excess energy to help others do the same. Money is a tool.

Okay, you now have a very simple model to improve your wealth and maybe even grow wealthy. And what about that equity thing? In 1920 there were about 12,000 millionaires in America, 6 of whom were Black. Today, there are about 22,000,000 millionaires and 340,000 are black. Not an equal amount, but a much higher ratio. But the task before us, is increasing overall income of American families **with no racial component.** Improvement will come from education and growing the pie. It will come as more of us take responsibility for our own living, then advancing, then greater success. Not everyone in America has the ability to grow their wealth with as little effort as possible, but the vast majority do.

National Poverty has become an industry, providing jobs in government and non-profits. Much of the media and academic elite have developed a campaign to make anyone with resources feel guilty about their status. This guilt is designed to get much of the country to **save** those with less. In the last five years this has become blatantly racial as those elites preach that simply being white makes you guilty of oppression. (The author had relatives who fought for the Union in the Civil War. I believe they would be furious.) I would argue that working to build wealth, employing others, and helping them start building wealth through innovation and expanding the pie offers something better. There is nothing racial about man helping man. Why would we as a society settle for helping people survive when we can give them the opportunity to thrive? Let's leave the guilt trip for those who keep telling people that society is stopping them from really succeeding. They should be ashamed.

I am reminded of my wife being involved in the creation of a Charter School that was focused on preserving and encouraging Native American culture and using that effort to encourage students who struggled a bit to succeed. In the beginning of the effort, a university professor, older and white drove the organizers' efforts. She proposed organizing around very bureaucratic structures with curriculum that focused on how to overcome victim status. She was a scholar of Native culture. For months the organizers struggled to finalize a plan and launch the school. One day a young native woman stood up and basically declared BS on the process. She objected to the academic views from people who knew what was best for native people. Within weeks the school's plan was finished, built around integrating native values with a clear need for the students to succeed in the world as it is. The school is wildly successful without anybody being saved. It is designed around the self-reliance that has allowed Native Americans to survive and thrive for generations.

You **own** yourself. Don't let anyone convince you that you can't thrive or that you are a victim. Pitch in and grow your wealth, create opportunity for others and then, like many before, **you can give it all away. Few people get more pleasure from taking than giving.**

How about that, the American economy in 40 pages. Is that all there is to it? No, but all that most people need to know for their daily lives. Economists, like many academics make it more complex, and debate grandiose issues, but they never agree.

> **'If all of the economists were lined up end to end, they'd never reach a conclusion.'**
>
> —George Bernard Shaw

So, let's move beyond the fundamentals of the economy. If the Capitalist System is so great, why aren't things better today? Why hasn't the nation created by the founding fathers done better? Let's discuss that history, the foundations of the country and the history of the last 250 years. What's in it for you? Perhaps you will see what has been working for you and society and things that need to be changed will come into sharper focus.

How we look at the world has changed, and not always for the better. Former Notre Dame and Hall of Fame football coach, Lou Holtz was asked what the difference in football players was today and 50 years ago. His answer, **"Simple, today's athletes talk about rights and privileges. And players 50 years ago talked about obligations and responsibilities."**

I use his comment to highlight how many people today misunderstand the founding principles of the country. Our history is remarkable in that it speaks to individual people doing remarkable things, not because they had to, but because it was right. Often that came with sacrifice, not benefits, obligations that would secure rights.

Leo Tolstoy once commented, "Everyone thinks of changing the world, but no one thinks of changing himself." Our current society is buried in social media, fears, and a desperate need for social approval. Society struggles with differences while at the same time celebrating them. We are confused. Interestingly, all but the amplification of social media has happened in prior periods and always thereafter the nation began to reach out to each other, to listen and to make one of our historic leaps forward. American history is one of shared threat, shared resolution, shared success, and shared world respect all standing on what liberated individuals did when necessary. It is also one of conflict. You own you; your opinions count as did your ancestors. They moved society using the tools provided by the founders.

A careful examination of the success in America is also an examination of the failures and problems in America. It is one of accepting progress. It is one that does not seek perfection, for perfection is based on current values, and as such is unattainable because values evolve. But the effort to always improve is one of America's most remarkable achievements. Natural Americans have never been satisfied with where they or we are.

So, here is a discussion of American history as it applies to the differences between Melody's feelings and the beliefs of this one greying guy.

"If you hear the dogs, keep going. If you see the torches in the woods, keep going. If there's shouting after you keep going. Don't ever stop. Keep going. If you want a taste of freedom, keep going."

–Harriet Tubman

6

AMERICAN HISTORY

*Our review of history and the impact on
all Americans, progress, or perfection*

HERE IS MY introduction to how American History might be looked at. While in college, I was engaged in student government. This was decades ago, but it seems little has changed. One of my colleagues, the son of an attorney from Seattle, and I used to debate on a lot of issues. He was very liberal, damned smart, and would probably have been in some elite university instead of a state school except for a couple of screwups in his early life. I was a classic state school enrollee, with a small subsidy from my mother's Social Security estate, full time work each summer and part time while in school.

The council was discussing waiving all academic and testing requirements to get into the college. My position was that we needed to make sure the new students enrolling had the skills to be successful, and if that took some remedial work due to failures in their K-12 education, that needed to be the focus. The colleague's position was that anyone who wanted to attend should be admitted. My concern was that setting up people to fail was not going to be good for their self-esteem and future life. Coming from a position of privilege, he didn't have a clue what I was talking about; (or worse, didn't care as long as his pet feelings were spared.)

My position prevailed and we sent our views to the state legislature. We pointed a finger at failures in the K-12 education system, especially in preparing lower income and minority students. (That's right, we were discussing this decades ago.) My colleague was really pissed, and his response was, "If we don't admit everybody the college is racist and should be destroyed."

There are a lot of folks who look at American society and the economy today and see problems. They assume, like my old debate foe, that the problems are institutional and because of that, the institutions need to be torn down. Okay, I understand how they feel. But I challenge you to think in addition to feel.

American society is a long way from perfect. But it doesn't take a deep dive to arrive at alternatives to tearing it down. First, you would have to ignore almost 250 years of progress…not perfection but progress. Second, you would have to understand that there are no historical examples of anything better. I've seen a dozen different presentations where a lecturer or leader challenged the audience to list five countries where communism or even direct socialism has succeeded. I've never seen that list get beyond the request. There aren't any. Try it yourself. Some nations, like England, Canada and Sweden have nationalized medicine which has both positives and negatives, (waiting lists for knee replacements can exceed two years), but their economies are pure capitalism.

How does this fit with the natural laws, working to create more wealth to take care of your family, and the fundamental, you own you? A nation allowed to build wealth, even one family at a time can build wealth for everyone; if the people are honorable and do it in a way that does not hurt their fellow citizens. If everyone does their part, the whole country prospers. Those of us who have moved up the **ladder** a bit realize that good partners and employees are critical to our own success. We also accept the natural law that "all men are created equal." That doesn't mean we all end up equal. It simply means we are all human beings, with the ability to succeed. (For the foreseeable future, some of us will have different paint jobs.)

With **liberty, by owning yourself**, you also have **great responsibility.**

HISTORICAL RACISM

(This seems to be the justification for a lot of complaints about America)

In a way, the United States didn't have a chance to avoid racism. Race was a seldom used concept in Europe through the 1500's. It was a term that separated people by geographic origin, sometimes by religious preference, (Jewish), and by characteristics. It had nothing to do with intellectual ability, physical performance, or human productivity or slavery.

By the 1600's European elites and philosophers were developing what they believed were "scientific" laws that allowed society to separate people by race, which in that period almost always included skin color. These scientific laws looked at head shape, cultural advancement, technological development, written language and other traits and customs. These weren't the laws of nature, but rather, laws about nature drawn from prejudiced observation. They were portrayed as facts much the same as early religious beliefs were portrayed as facts; (the sun revolves around the earth.)

Over the next two centuries the students of those philosophers declared that people with white skin were superior to those of other colors. That because of their "superior" intelligence, culture, and religions they should be the dominant race. Tragically this was accepted almost all over the world. People of color who were being subjugated and defeated in warfare by superior technology in their own lands were forced to accept that they could not compete. They did not acknowledge that they were less as human beings, only that they could not protect their lands, families, religions, and culture from more technically advanced European armies. Many, for their cultures to survive, accepted European dominance, even in the Americas.

By the early 1600's it was widely accepted that Africans, captured by other Africans in warfare and raids, often brokered by Arabs, were inferior to the point that they could be enslaved as workers even though they were not captured in warfare. Remember the natural law, create wealth with as little effort as possible? Well, it took a lot less effort to force inferior people who had been sold by other black people to work in the fields than do it yourself.

Slavery itself is as old as organized civilization. Up until the 1600's slaves were not defined by race, only by military might. Perhaps 4,000 years of slavery preceded the creation of the United States. The Romans practiced slavery. Russia and the Slavic states had centuries of slavery history as did the Crimea and the Barbary Coast of Africa. Christian, Ottoman, Islamic nations practiced slavery. The Spanish empire took slavery everywhere they sailed. Slavery was even part of what some societies called blood tax, where children were taken from parents and sold into slavery because the parents could not pay their taxes. Asian societies practiced slavery, again with most slaves captured in warfare. No one cared what color a slave's skin was.

African and American indigenous groups captured people from other tribes and put them to work. Some could potentially become tribal members, but all would work or starve. In the seventeenth and eighteenth centuries, more than 300,000 white people were shipped to America as slaves. Some were criminals, others street urchins, some were duped into becoming indentured servants, unaware that once in the new world they could be bought and sold as property. The first white people sent to colonize Australia were white criminal slaves.

Slave labor was cheap and helped a lot of people all over the world, from many ethnic groups improve their personal and family wealth with a lot less effort than doing it themselves. **Remember, that before capitalism, the only path to wealth was to steal it or enslave others to work for you.** The adoption of capitalism was one of the essential processes that eventually made slavery obsolete, by unchaining the power of innovation, especially in technology. That didn't happen overnight.

But race became a clear delineator of slavery in the new world. And one thing was universal of all slaves, they did **not own** themselves. That did not mean that they accepted their fate. Slaves were a lot of trouble. Many mastered ways of fighting back. They were always a threat. Slave rebellions in southern states spilled both black and white blood. The carnage of the slave rebellion in Haiti, which ended with the nation's independence from France in 1803 shocked and terrified the American south. (France demanded and collected reparations from Haiti for decades, to compensate the French slave owners for the loss of their human property.) In effect the newly independent leaders of Haiti paid for their freedom in order for the nation to become independent.

Slaves were important; they supplied the manpower for much of the economic expansion of the early Americas. I remember an economics professor in college who was convinced that slavery was never really economical. He was desperate to find a justification for his feelings about slavery. The fact is, that slaves were the tractors, the graders, the hay rakes, cotton planters and harvesters, the grain combines of American economic expansion. They built buildings, they used picks and shovels to create roads. The only alternative was to pay people wages to do the work, but there were not many entry level wage citizens. Slavery was not only economically justified; it was really important to the early economic success of America, as it was across the globe.

Slaves were especially valuable in agriculture where they could not only tend crops, but also grow enough to feed themselves.

(Imagine your John Deere tractor creating all the fuel it uses). In the 1800's, the number of slaves in the Caribbean states had grown so much that food crops could not support the population. A huge industry grew up in New England to ship salted fish to the Caribbean countries to keep the slaves from starving. Even abolitionist New Englanders participated arguing that if they did not, a lot of people would starve.

Slaves were a huge financial investment and an asset to the owners. In some cases, the slaves employed by an enterprise were worth more than the real estate where they worked. But throughout the early history of the Americas there was also a strong movement to end slavery.

There is a great deal of discussion now over Slavery being the catalyst for the American revolution. The 1619 project of the New York Times argues that that Americans only revolted from England because the English were about to abolish slavery and that would have carried over into their colonies. This seems to be a conclusion in search of a factual argument. The English parliament didn't even begin debating the elimination of slavery until two decades after the American Revolution. But the English, Dutch, Spanish and French all brought slavery with them to the new world. The Danish were small time players in the slave trade, but among the most brutal. By the time the American Civil War broke out, there were about 4 million slaves, most of them black, helping people grow more wealth in America. Some of them were descendants of slaves. Many were purchased off from auction blocks or from other slave owners. Very few were recent arrivals from Africa.

Anyone who believes that men naturally want to create more wealth can understand that a single man with a hoe can work a lot less land than a man with two slaves helping. Slavery was practiced for about 230 of the 500 years after the first Europeans came to the new world. No one really knows how long the original native people used the practice.

Slavery ended in America 166 years ago, that is just over five historical generations. Some are of the opinion that America must compensate the victims of slavery. The number of black people has grown from 4 million to 41 million in those 166 years, but as of today there is not a single former slave alive in the country. One of my favorite stories is from the second year after the end of the Civil War. A plantation owner begged his former top slave to come back and work for him. The slave sent him a bill for 22 years of past wages with a note that he would consider it after payment was received. The request from a former slave makes a lot of sense. Compensation to his great, great, great granddaughter is more questionable. In fact, it is nonsense.

Perhaps we can change the perception of slavery. Not the one that makes it clear that it was wrong and an abomination. No, the one where decedents of slaves somehow still feel shame, they too are victims. The black slaves that worked without compensation, suffering abuse and humiliation through the mid 1800's, were critical to building the foundation of the country. Their resourcefulness and **resilience** in the face of horrid conditions is, at least to me, a really uplifting part of our history. The nation needs to clearly applaud the efforts, resilience, and contribution of its first black members. Only in the last couple of decades are the stories of the rebels among the slaves being told. Any critical examination of history documents reveals this nation's extraordinary efforts to heal the wounds of slavery. It also will shine a spotlight on the nation's failures.

THE REVOLUTIONARY WAR

Okay, so what fueled the revolution against the British, if it wasn't slavery? For two and a half centuries historians studying the papers of the founding fathers wrote that it all boiled down to "you don't own me." Forgive me, but the next couple of chapters will touch on that time in America's history, but unlike history in school, we will look at the impact on the American people, not government or the military.

This book began with a discussion about Thomas Paine's book, COMMON SENSE. If you haven't actually read it, it should be on your immediate to do list. Paine was a Brit who came to America at the invitation of Ben Franklin. He was a social revolutionary in England and brought his beliefs with him to the new world. COMMON SENSE was a small pamphlet that came out as tensions rose between the colonists and England. It became one of the most widely read books in the world and is credited with sparking common citizen revolution against oppressive monarchy in America and across Europe and the globe. Paine had only been in America for a few months when he wrote it.

There were real differences between the Americans and their British masters, even though colonists were supposedly British citizens. Most differences were centered around massive taxes imposed by the British government on the colonies. Britain had been engaged in extensive warfare in Europe, and even in the Americas for years and pressed the colonists for the money to pay off the Crown's debts. Taxes went through the roof. The colonies were prohibited from electing their own governors. Colonists objected to taxation without having any representation in parliament. British law treated the colonists as lesser citizens. British soldiers bullied and humiliated Americans. Americans were prohibited from manufacturing goods that real English citizens made and wanted to sell to the colonies. While people in England were steadily stripping power over their lives from the King, the government they created worked with the King to hold down colonists' ambitions and dreams.

Eventually the discourse devolved into protest and civil disobedience. Colonists began harassing British troops who had harassed them for years. We all know about the BOSTON TEA PARTY. Americans objected to the crown's rules that made England the only country that the Americans could trade with. The citizens refused to comply. The British monarch responded by sending troops into the streets of Boston, forcing the citizens to house and feed the soldiers in their own homes. A majority of the citizens just wanted to remedy the Monarch's injustices. They were okay with remaining British citizens. But the government began a campaign of repression that just inflamed the people. No one really knew what to do. Attempts to negotiate with the government were failing. All attempts to appeal to the King were rebuffed.

Paine, who was a magazine editor at the time, put pen to paper and wrote COMMON SENSE. The book laid out four arguments for American Independence.

1. The history of mankind

    Individual men, isolated, independent, free, create free societies as they form more complex government. Without checks and balances those governments often develop anti-social elements and policies. Those governments become what many consider a necessary evil, and sometimes an intolerable evil.

2. Anti-monarchy

    There is no logical, biological, or moral right to hereditary leadership. Societies create leaders to coordinate their efforts and safety. You follow a leader for three reasons:

    - You fear them (monarchy)
    - You follow their intellect (enlightened)
    - Your life or livelihood depend on them

    When leaders no longer make life better, or worse threaten it, society has a right to change them.

3. Focus on the colonies and their societies:
    - The break with England is inevitable and justified;
    - Independence is a shield against corrupt or antagonistic foreign monarchs or governments;
    - Separation allows each of the 13 colonies to emphasize their strengths while allowing America to become a trading hub to the world without foreign entanglements; and
    - Separation opens the door to freedom loving refugees in an empty land.

4. To succeed in a rebellion against England, the rest of the world needed to see and understand the injustices and to believe that America intended to win its independence. The people needed to advertise their clear intent and goal and that would open the door to foreign help and recognition. They needed a plan.

If the American public had seen any real progress toward reconciling the injustices they felt, there is a very good chance that the American Revolution would not have happened, at least not at that time. But there was no progress, nothing got better, and the King cracked down.

(We know that some will look at the 'empty land' and ask, what about the Native Americans? Remember that this was the 1770's and 'educated' people all knew that white people were superior and as such, the Indian's inefficient use of land was wasteful. This is history and as such is not for any of us to like, but to understand and learn from. Because it takes place in a set time it is not open to revision.)

Paine's arguments refer to "natural laws" which at the time were a combination of actual biological/physical laws and the teachings of the Christian Church. These Natural Americans believed that they had natural rights to grow their wealth and take care of their families. They lived in a time that allowed many to use the labors of others without paying for their time through the institution of slavery. But only a small percentage of Citizens owned slaves. Many of their peers were working to end the practice. All were willing to risk everything to poke the king in the eye and snarl, **you don't own me.**

So, Paine's arguments led perhaps a third of the population to favor separation from England. Perhaps another 20% would never agree to separation and the remaining population took a wait and see attitude. Once hostilities began, those opposing separation supported the English, actually joining their military efforts. Many of those in the middle eventually supported the cause of independence.

The Declaration of Independence was signed by 56 men, all white. At that time the society across the world granted almost all governmental power to men. Forty-one owned slaves, but there were also ardent abolitionists. Twenty-three were lawyers, eleven were merchants, many were farmers or plantation owners, all were educated. None were black or Native American, but that does not make them stupid or wrong.

During the war, five of these men were captured and tortured as rebels. Nine died in the fighting. Two lost sons. All but thirteen saw their business interests destroyed in the war. Constant movement to stay ahead of British troops sent out to capture them broke up families. Some lost wives and children. Most lost their homes. Of the 56, only 13 maintained most of their wealth and lives. Many eventually died penniless.

Think about the commitment of these men who paid a terrible price to engage the most powerful nation and army in the world at the time. Consider their commitment when your feelings gnaw at you when you look at illegal immigrants from Latin America. Some there, face government persecution and risks from criminals. Some face government policy that pits the wealthy against the citizens.

They rush to the United States where our country's citizens gave so much to throw off similar persecution and have shed blood for 200 years to protect what the founders built. None of the people flooding our southern border face a foe in their own countries that is as fierce as Britain in the 1700's. Why do they not fight for their own country, even if it means sacrifice? Six of ten people crossing our border are men of military age, and there are millions of them, all claiming persecution. Perhaps they can fix their own countries and build powerful, fair, honorable nations in their homeland. Perhaps we are a bit too quick to extend a hand. **Albert Einstein's comment, "I am thankful to all of those who said no, because of them, I did it myself**, is at least worthy of consideration.

The American founders knew the risk when they signed and many paid a terrible price, but the survivors and their peers went on to create the United States of America and to write a constitution that is a model for the world, and a process for modifying the Constitution that has been used 27 times. Among the initial amendments were those that created what we know as the Bill of Rights. The American society has used the amendment process to address issues never considered by the founding fathers and to alter their original intent as society changed. (Today liberal thinkers, growing frustrated that they cannot get congress to enact policies they favor, because the Constitution does not support those positions, have pushed for reformist judges who reinterpret the Constitution or simply argue that it does not apply.)

Melody, your comments on the Constitution strongly indicated that you felt it was obsolete, that the problems it addressed were very different than today. The rest of this chapter addresses those concerns.

Perhaps just as important, the American Revolution, and the adoption of the Constitution and the first elections in 1789 guaranteed white men the right to grow their wealth and do it with as little effort as possible. The drag of the monarchy was eliminated.

The economy of the United States took off. So good for those old white men, you say. It was also the beginning of the march toward equal rights beyond the traditional rights of white men. Those men risked everything, and many gave everything to scream to the world, **you don't own me**.

The war ended in 1783 and the Constitution was adopted in 1789. In 1794 those same men, many who owned slaves passed the Slave Trade Act making it illegal for American ships to engage in the international slave trade. (Five northern states made slavery illegal immediately.) Over the next five years the national act was strengthened repeatedly, but the relatively weak central government struggled to enforce it. To a large degree it worked as slave transport remained mostly a European industry.

Many of those same men passed a law making it illegal to import slaves in 1807. Again, it was difficult to enforce, but ships caught bringing slaves into the country were impounded and the crews and owners fined heavily. People who tipped federal authorities could be awarded ownership of seized ships. Other provisions made it illegal to invest in the slave trade and outlawed some employment in the slave industry.

The practice of slavery was central to much of the debate in the early days of Congress. By 1820, the Missouri Compromise admitted Missouri into the Union as a slave state and Maine as a free state and laid the groundwork for the elimination of slavery in the country. In the northern states, substantial populations of free black men and women were taking their place building their own wealth. In the southern states, slavery persisted, and the practice evolved to the point where some free black men were buying slaves.

One place where there was substantial equality between the races was in the American Navy where white and black worked side by side beginning with the Revolutionary War, both races sharing the same jobs.

The American Revolution was not fought over slavery. It was, however, a clear starting point for the government recognizing that natural law gives us the right to build our wealth, including the acquisition of property through work. It was also the clear starting point for recognition that a European monarch did not own the American people and laid the groundwork that American people do not own other American people no matter what color they are.

One of the things that led to this book was a full acceptance that with the rights to build wealth, to own yourself and what you earn, comes a clear understanding that it brings with it the understanding that Americans **honor other Americans and with great freedom comes great responsibility**. This is the underpinning for the Constitution, and the economy including the society that it encouraged.

From the end of the Revolutionary War in September of 1783, this country has been built on liberty and freedom. Those two things do not preclude equality, nor do they create it. Liberty and Freedom encourage each one of us to be masters of ourselves; to reach for the gold. Liberty does not provide for some to share in what they do not produce. Nor does it allow for artificial barriers to another American's creation of wealth for themselves and their families. The founding fathers realized that growing the economy was critical to the survival and success of the nation. They argued to create equal opportunity, not equity.

Yet, as government has grown, many barriers have crept into our society. Even major efforts by Americans to overcome those barriers haven't yielded immediate results. In fact, some of the most targeted efforts have failed. But just like the outline on how you can succeed in the American capitalist economy, failure just means that something didn't work. Remember Milton Friedman's comments from earlier in the book. Judge government programs by their results, not their intentions. We should learn from that and then keep on trying.

You own you. Try, try, again. **We own us.** We keep on getting better.

THE AMERICAN CIVIL WAR

The differences between the southern and northern states continued, from the time of the original Constitution into the mid 1850's. Many leaders of the southern states had been opposed to the creation of a strong central government fearing interference with their personal lives, local and state government, and their livelihood. The Bill of Rights was substantially added to the Constitution as a compromise to those who feared that a strong central government might run roughshod over its citizens rights. The very Bill of Rights that provides legal precedence for racial justice was, paradoxically championed by southern politicians. The compromises on slavery acknowledged that slavery was more important in the agrarian south than the industrializing northern states. For many who owned slaves as beasts of burden it was a real stretch to look at those beasts as equal human beings. Yet the country had legislated from the 1820's on, that slavery would be abolished.

Many today look at the southerners claim that the Civil War was fought over States Rights. Surely, they say, the central theme was slavery. To much of the South, especially the political elite, there was no difference in those two issues.

The abolitionist north was constantly pressing for an immediate end to slavery, believing it morally evil. The southern landed class saw no alternative to slaves working the fields. Technology, like automated seed planters were slowly coming into existence, but to the South there was no alternative to slavery if the plantation life was to continue to exist.

Abraham Lincoln began practicing law as a junior partner in a firm where the senior partner was a devout abolitionist. The unwillingness of the earlier Whig party to directly attack slavery had led to its demise in the north and replacement with a stridently anti-slavery Republican Party. Lincoln's election to the presidency sent a clear message to the southern leadership. Slavery was really going to end.

We won't rehash the Civil War here. But a couple of issues with today's narrative stand out. One is that anyone who had ever owned slaves was and is evil. It's easy to take our modern values and judge people who had spent their entire lives in a society where slavery was an everyday part of life, as it had been for 4,000 years. Many of those slave holders were among the first to free their slaves and renounce the practice and then worked hard to help freed men. They led the Union army in the Civil War. They gave up sons and neighbors, tens of thousands of them in the war. The Christian faith teaches forgiveness as one of its most important tenants.

Some challenge Lincoln because he openly stated early in the war that he was fighting to preserve the Union, not free the slaves. Those who criticize his musings forget that if he had not preserved the Union, the South would have broken away leaving the millions of slaves under a government where there was no pressure to end slavery. They also ignore that Lincoln was a committed abolitionist.

The thirteenth amendment to the Constitution documented what Lincoln started with the Emancipation Proclamation, it freed all the slaves and gave them some basic rights. The Emancipation Proclamation only freed southern slaves, not those in "Yankee" states. What the end of the war also did was crush the economy of the south. Many southerners' entire net worth was in slaves, and in a matter of months they were broke. The plantations could not plant or harvest without workers. Many southerners had developed close relationships with slaves over the years, but a lot of them still saw slaves as beasts of burden, not fellow citizens. Poor southern white people, and there were a lot of them after the war decimated southern industry, saw the newly freed black people as low-cost labor that would replace them in their already starvation wage jobs. Over the years of the war, the southern economy shrunk by as much as 80%.

The only people in the South, at the end of the war, who could build their wealth with little effort were northerners with money who took advantage of the desperate economy in the South by buying properties from the destitute former owners for pennies on the dollar. In some places where that didn't work, they helped former slaves become political leaders in communities, where former rebels were prevented from holding office. These black legislators, protected by federal troops, then orchestrated tax increases on already stretched landowners. Their northern benefactors then bought the properties as they were sold for unpaid taxes.

To many in the North nothing was too terrible for the defeated south. But to others who took the longer view that the nation needed to heal its divide, such practices were abhorrent. (For those of you who today believe that anyone remotely connected to historical slavery is abhorrent and should be erased, imagine if the post-Civil War days were managed by people who believed that. We might still be fighting a guerilla war a century and a half later instead of reconciling.) There is a lot of hatred for people like Robert E. Lee, who was offered command of the Union Army when the Civil War erupted but resigned from the northern army because he could not "fight against my neighbors and friends." He was already an American war hero from the Mexican War, and when it was clear that the war was lost, he surrendered his army and ordered Southern soldiers not to fight a guerilla war against the North so that the nation could heal.

The North used the power of its military to try to walk the line between punishment and reconciliation in the early days of reconstruction. The creation of schools for former slaves was encouraged. Former slaves moved into the trades and business. Two out of five 'cowboys' on the western frontier in the next decades were former slaves. The military aggressively recruited black service members.

Former slaves rejoiced in truly recognizing **Nobody Owns Me.** They were free for the first time to build personal wealth for themselves and their families.

Black merchants, farmers, craftsmen began to succeed in the former southern states. Southern elites still considered them lower class humans but could do little to block their advancement because of tens of thousands of federal troops patrolling the south. Initially several states sent black representatives to congress, all Republicans. This effort was assisted by a constitutional amendment that made former rebels unable to run for office. Even those southerners who had renounced the rebellion and worked with northern appointed officials toward reconstruction and human rights for freed slaves couldn't run for office. By the end of the war most white southerners, while not supporting the causes of the rebellion, also didn't support northern occupation; few whites were qualified for office. To many southerners, life became showing the North that it didn't own them.

Over the next decade, the policy against white southern leadership in office eroded and the old-line Democratic Party slowly reemerged. With their return to power, those opposed to equal rights for freed slaves emerged, most notable, the Ku Klux Klan or KKK. As the north pushed for integration of new black citizens into the society, those who were still bitter over losing the Civil War and their treatment in the early days of reconstruction pushed back. By the election of 1876, twenty years later the nation stood at the doorstep of a second civil war.

That election pitted Republican Rutherford B. Hayes against Democrat Samuel Tilden, and because of obviously tainted voting tabulations in five states, neither could muster a majority of electoral college votes. There was no president-elect and the two sides found no middle ground to arrive at a solution. The Republicans had controlled the Federal Government for almost a quarter century, and the Democrats, mostly southern, felt that the North was still running their lives through military presence in the South. Eventually a compromise was reached. Enough votes were awarded to Hayes for the Republican to become President, while Hayes and the Republicans agreed to remove all troops from the South.

Over the next 80 years, freed slaves substantially improved their lives, both through new lives in the North and by persisting under very difficult circumstances in the South. In many northern states they achieved equal status in citizenship including running for office and voting. The South, still chaffing from their failure and humiliation during reconstruction, enacted laws that severely limited Black access to office and voting rights. Many, especially poor whites, reacted to black economic success with jealousy and envy, believing that much of that success had only come from the North tilting the scales in favor of former slaves. They had a point. Many of these same restrictions were extended to other groups, like Native Americans. As disgruntled southerners with no economic stake in the south spread into newly developing western territories, many brought their attitude about race with them. Northerners moving into the same territories remained abolitionists.

Life for former slaves was better. **You don't own me** was better than being a slave, but economic progress was difficult and sometimes met with violent repression. Most former slaves living in the South were denied education, good jobs, and justice. By the 1950's with the integration of the American military, a larger group of newly wealthy Black Americans created new education and business opportunities for their struggling neighbors, progress toward economic integration was flourishing. A strong black middle class was developing, especially in the South where colored businesspeople catered to other colored people who had limited access to transportation, restaurants, and hotels. They emphasized the differences between southern white and black tastes and cultures. They found a problem, used their efforts and innovation to solve it and launched themselves toward building wealth. As they expanded, they hired workers to increase their wealth with less effort. Black owned business catered to black citizens who had limited access to white owned facilities. Still in the South, political access was stifled.

Southern Democrats were dragged into efforts to pass landmark civil rights legislation in the 1950's and 1960's by Northerners who again threatened and used military intervention in the South, troops literally at the schools in the South. That legislation focused on voting rights and education, but also on providing equal access for all races to public accommodations including stores, restaurants, transportation, and hotels. Note that earlier in the book we made some observations about government intervention and unintended consequences. The public accommodations part of the civil rights legislation opened white owned transportation, food services and hotels to black citizens, and they flocked to them. Within ten years, the percentage of middle-class black citizens collapsed as many black owned businesses could not connect to white citizens while their historic clientele took advantage of opportunities they had never had before and abandoned black owned business.

At the same time the rapid expansion of manufacturing in the north drew huge numbers of black citizens from the South for high paying jobs in the North. Mobility created opportunity and tens of thousands of black citizens moved north to create wealth for themselves and families.

The loss of black middle-class as black businessmen failed and was eventually replaced by black craftsmen working in factories. New opportunities opened up through civil rights movements and legislation sparked an expansion of new black entrepreneurs. In the 100 years following the end of the Civil War, the nation saw economic growth among the families of former slaves. Remember, they started with nothing. Seizing the opportunity to grow wealth, many moved north.

But two things, while improved, were still stifling success. First, in the South, the political elite openly opposed full integration.

Second in the North, new black families moving into what had been all white neighborhoods surprised and worried even white people who had supported their definition of racial justice. Many northerners had never known any black citizens. Fear of these new neighbors and their impact on local economies was widespread.

In the South, economic growth evolved to become dependent on black workers. In both the South and the North, fear over what successful black families might do to property values led real estate developers and communities to develop restrictive property covenants that kept non-whites from free access to housing and at the same time, banks worried about their loan portfolios and developed what they call redlining policies. These policies made it difficult for people in largely non-white communities to get bank loans. With homes in those areas harder to finance, they became harder to sell. This held down the values of these homes at a time when homes across America were appreciating rapidly in value. A home's increased value is still one of the most important components of building wealth for your family. You increase your wealth with very little effort. Racially based zoning, restrictive real estate covenants and red lining expanded.

Bluntly, real American values and the opportunity to grow wealth, with as little effort as possible were being defeated as some forgot the other parts of the American agreement. The rights of fellow Americans were not honored. Regulatory restrictions that stifled some Americans' ability to create wealth, and grow the pie hurt them and all of us.

How did government respond? Instead of just eliminating the blockages and getting out of the way, they developed a mind-boggling array of programs, that instead of just freeing up and encouraging the citizens' ability to take care of themselves, instead set out to help victims. Justified by historical wrongs, the government began paying people enough to survive. It created programs of training and forced business to recruit people of color. But many of those recruited came out of a very different culture, they struggled to connect with or even understand business issues. I personally watched with anguish the early days of equal opportunity employment as bright young people ran headlong into language, business practices, and cultural values that they struggled to understand. When stressed they tended to go talk about a product, service, or company without really understanding that business purchases and improvement are all based on the organization's **need**. Business does not make decisions based on the features of a product, but instead considers if trading wealth for a product will solve a business problem. Cultural differences created listening and comprehension difficulties. I am not convinced that EEO was not positive in the long run but observed a lot of unprepared people shake their heads and walk away thinking they were failures. Interestingly, the one group who defied this observation were people who had served in the military. Frankly they were better listeners, more disciplined and more comfortable with people from differing backgrounds.

Between 1865 and 2006 the Federal Government passed 14 major civil rights acts and constitutional amendments. Since the Civil Rights Act of 1964, the government has spent 22 trillion dollars on programs to help victims, the vast majority on programs paid attention to people of color. To put this into perspective, if you divide the expenditure by the number of black Americans in 1970, the amount totals more than 1 million dollars each.

The result should be obvious to all of us now. Over the last four decades the government has taxed producers, and even worse, borrowed money, trillions of dollars to compensate people to not participate in the most powerful economy on earth. While this paid some rent and put food on the table it did little except to pay them **not** to be part of the success. As the rust belt grew, more and more people were paid just enough so that they would not fully take part in an economy that was going in new directions, in new locations, requiring new skills. Black citizens moved North in the 1940's and 1950's to find greater opportunity. Today government pays people to stay where they are even though economic opportunity may be across the country. Incredibly the people pushing these payoff strategies have worked tirelessly to convince the recipients that they should support a government that pays them to survive instead of thrive. We all need to challenge this. Those affected should ask the question; **does government now own me? If you are substantially dependent on Government, the answer may be yes.**

Government has not been very successful in helping people thrive.

What does this mean in real numbers, to real people? In 1960, 22% of Americans lived below the poverty level. 17% of whites, (30,000,000) were below the poverty level and 55% of black Americans (10,000,000) were considered impoverished based on numbers from the census bureau.

In 2020, America had cut the poverty percentages in half, now only 11.4% of the population lived below the poverty level. 8.2% of whites (17,000,000) fell into that category, while 19% of black Americans (8,000,000) lived below the official poverty level.

In total numbers, it's important to consider that in the same period, the white population increased by 46,000,000 or 29%. The black population increased by 22,000,000 or 210%. White families had fewer children and white immigration was minimal. The black population increased through immigration with perhaps as many as 20% of the population new since the 1960's. Of greater impact, the number of black offspring has increased by almost 100%.

Impoverished black citizens have decreased from 10M to 8M despite a more than doubling of the population, while white poverty has decreased from 30M to 17M in great part to the stability of the population. Certainly, cultural differences contribute to this. Increased average black family wealth, over these 50 years, yielded much smaller pieces for Black Americans than their white neighbors. Created family wealth was divided by more family members. Early redlining and property restrictions held down the value of black owned property. But for both black and white, there is another troubling factor.

We're not criticizing family structure here. But you cannot ignore one statistic. In 1964, 24% of black children and 3.1% of white children were born into single parent families. By 1990 that had risen to 64% of black children and 18% of white children. The opportunity to grow family wealth in a single parent household is diminished by perhaps as much as 80% in comparison to two parent households.

Today, with the war on energy, we are creating a new class of those left out. These are people in viable economic industries who are being pushed out of their jobs and the middle class because of politics. You wonder why so many blue-collar white people have become politically charged. Imagine being told that you are bad just because a job that may have supported a good living for generations is now politically incorrect. If you work in coal, you obviously hate the environment. Those workers see the majority of remedial programs pointed at the inner city and people of color and feel left out. They are being left out and they are now pariahs to many. They aren't demonstrating or rioting, and nobody is listening to them. Their rich heritage of self-reliance is being replaced by depression and substance abuse.

There are still too many poor in the country. In 2022 when the entire nation is screaming for employees, something other than government poverty programs is required as the answer. The following sentences will probably piss off a lot of folks, but this book is being written in a way to stick a finger in the eye of cancel culture on both the left and right.

The K-12 education system needs to make three fundamental changes. First it needs to completely abandon social progress and create curriculum that unleashes the power of those who are prepared; and offer real remedial help to those who are not. Second, it needs to focus tax dollars on preparing citizen and legal immigrant children for success. (There is room for assisting Dreamers in this policy, but we need to realize that it is terribly diluting to the education budget and infrastructure to be plugging students with 50 different base languages into the same classrooms.) Finally, we need to reject the educational elites focus on college. We need to support the prepared and offer support to get the rest prepared to move up the ladder. The idea of advancement based on your age needs to be replaced with advancement based on achievement.

Years ago, I participated in a forum on education. It was made up of about 60% local business executives, 20% people from non-profit programs and 20% from education. Of the 20% from education perhaps two dozen were from the university environment. At the time I was representing a small airline and flight school. Along with dozens from trucking, communications, heavy construction, and other business we came to plead the case for high school and initial years of college to refocus on preparing students for hands-on jobs. The group put together a policy that made that type of preparation one of its foremost recommendations. At that point, several of the university people became incensed. One, a dean from a university stood up and chastised the group for being so shortsighted. I am paraphrasing here, but the jest of his comments went something like this. "If you don't prepare students for a university education, including laying the groundwork for advanced degrees, you are failing them and the community and I for one will not add my name to such nonsense."

What utter and complete arrogance. That elitist attitude included the process of hijacking parental responsibility to prepare children for life, the society, and the changing economy.

Thomas Sowell, the economist and social theorist from Stanford University's Hoover Institute observed, "The problem isn't that Johnny can't read. The problem isn't even that

Johnny can't think. The problem is that Johnny doesn't know what thinking is; he confuses it with feeling."

The American educational system should not eliminate teaching social concerns, but it needs to be secondary to offering knowledge and the ability to use that knowledge to make decisions, to think. We need to refocus on core studies and encourage well educated people, even those educated in trades, to use their own ability to think about their place in society and their responsibility.

The nation needs to refocus on manufacturing and other blue-collar industries including the fossil fuel industry by abandoning the political correctness and sloganeering and offering real assistance to making industry as clean as possible with as much growth potential as possible. We need to accept that other than a rose, or a leaping rainbow trout, or perhaps for a poem or two, there is no perfection in the world. There is progress and every few years, some breakthrough changes the entire argument. Perfection is best left to deities beyond man and those they bless with remarkable life and world changing ideas.

History in the United Sates is one of consistent, measurable, and meaningful progress for all Natural Americans. We are a multiracial, multicultural, and multilingual society in a world that has struggled to avoid political problems by demanding conformity. In 2022 Canada, one of the former British colonies to gain independence without warfare or the struggles of civil disobedience had declared that anyone who disagrees with the elite political class is a rebel. They need to be put in their place. Canada will never be the same again. China imprisons anyone who disagrees with the policies of the CCP. They put millions into reeducation camps. Cuba is one of the few examples of a multiracial nation, where everyone is equally poor and where no dissent is possible, and people are fleeing.

The USA remains the beacon to the world. A significant part of the American citizenry is dissatisfied with our progress. That's great, they have that right, maybe even an obligation, but instead of tearing their neighbor and the institutions down, they might focus that energy on helping more prepare for and participate in what has worked for 200 years.

I hope that Melody and the readers recognize that we all are looking for a process to arrive at much the same place. We all want everyone to have the opportunity to become Natural Americans, to succeed in creating wealth for themselves and their families. As they become more skilled and knowledgeable, we would like them to increase that wealth with less effort and at the same time create opportunity for others.

The Capitalist economic model of the United States offers extraordinary opportunity to do just that, but only if the nation unlocks the chains constraining it and lets it soar. The history of the United States is a two-hundred-year book of progress, some of it a stop and start again progress. Citizens have called on government to establish rules and policy to help citizens. Often, they have created new rules that interfere with the desired success. The history is one of the citizens doing a better job of lifting all of us than government has done.

The social and especially legal system, as originally envisioned, could have worked wonders for all. But the original rules and policies set down in the Constitution as amended have been twisted to meet short term political values. The legal system has added legal rules on behalf of some of us, only to run into the quagmire of the laws of unintended consequences. We will discuss this in the next chapter.

> "In matters of conscience the law of the majority has no place."
>
> –Mahatma Gandhi

7

YOU, ME, AND SOCIETY UNDER THE LAW

*Our discussion of the legal system and
society, intentions, or results*

As NOTED IN the last chapter, there are still about 33,000,000 Americans living at or near the poverty level. The achievements of many non-white leaders in the country have been at best footnotes to our history. Racism in the legal system, especially as it affects the use of force is rare, but still unacceptable. What I think we would disagree on, is what to do about the problems, which must begin with the causes. Let's start with a really simplified history of man's creation of society. (This analysis is basic, but it is important. It took me 40 years to even consider this, but it changed how I look at life.)

SOCIETY

In the beginning there was only man and woman. They figured out how much fun it was to make more humans and the result, their immediate family. They hunted, gathered, and protected themselves from all manner of threats. Everyone participated in every activity to stay alive, which was a challenge as a lot of creatures looked at man as food. As noted in the second chapter of this book, the single greatest goal of each individual was to control the most territory to hunt and gather as much as possible in order to raise offspring who in turn would raise offspring. Old age in these groups was thirty-five. **Everyone owned themselves and had ownership responsibilities only to themselves and their tiny group.**

As families grouped together, they found that some people were more skilled at certain things and over a period developed group dynamics that allowed the best hunters to do that while others focused on preparing clothing, building shelters, or gathering firewood and food. When threatened the group defended itself. Everyone had a say and the group depended on each doing his best at whatever he or she was skilled at. **Remember this thought.** Government was the group getting together and making decisions, a direct democracy. **Here too, everyone owned themselves.**

With the development of agriculture and more sophisticated forms of hunter gather societies, people began to gather into larger groups. Economically, it was more efficient to have people more developed in some skills or trades work on those tasks while other people did other jobs. In small socio-economic groups, coordination was still as simple as getting the group together and dividing up the jobs necessary to provide food clothing and shelter. Many of these groups, located where fish and game stocks made food gathering reliable, developed strong art and cultures with their free time. Across the board in these communities, a little extra allowed the development of specialists in religion and culture. At this level, when threatened the group defended its members. **People in the group had sacrificed a little bit of independence but still owned themselves. With liberty they were free to leave if they chose.**

More people came together into larger communities, groups where it was impossible for the entire band to get together and agree on what needed to be done and by whom. This is where the trouble started. Initially it was one member of each household who would participate in a group meeting to divide up responsibilities among families and specific people. Most of these communities were patriarchal, but across the globe some were matriarchal. As long as everyone did their job, the system worked fairly well. But when someone failed to live up to their responsibilities, the group suffered, and others needed to be diverted from their tasks to fill the gap. Eventually squabbling broke out among the families. To remedy this, it was agreed that there needed to be an arbitrator which evolved into a leader. This was a **Representative Democracy** in its most basic form.

Laws were created to deal with what happens if someone does not do what they agree to do or are required to do for the benefit of the society. Laws were created so that those who choose to create personal wealth by taking that of others in the group could be punished.

Remember Thomas Paine's thoughts on leadership. You follow a leader because you fear them, or you follow their intellect, or your life or livelihood depend on them. Following their intellect works well, but either of the other, if not kept in check, often evolves into the **leader owning you.**

The next step in societal development can and did, in many cases, really upset the apple cart for individual ownership. More complex societies, the kind that needed roads and public granaries, public baths, and standing militaries to defend against neighbor groups trying to take what they had, allowed its leaders to develop governments to manage all of these functions. An all-powerful leader could impose taxes on the citizens, overrule long standing traditions on how to deal with work allocation and penalties for nonperformance, hurting others or taking what was theirs. Of course, most of these impositions did not apply to the elites. Almost universally these leadership positions became hereditary. Unless you were well up in the King or Queen's circle or a critical piece of the newly formed bureaucracy, your personal freedoms were curtailed. Any attempt to create real personal wealth for yourself and family was often arbitrarily seized by the leader. They and their cronies grew wealthy with little effort as they commanded their citizens. In many of these societies, favored bureaucrats, such as tax collectors, were allocated wealth well beyond their contribution to the society; **they owned you.** Where you were from or the color of your skin mattered little. You were not free to create wealth and often didn't even benefit from innovation that made the work easier, so there was little incentive to create better ways of doing things.

This form of government evolved into what we historically refer to as monarchy. It was exactly the form of government that led to the excesses fueling the fire of the American Revolution, a form of authoritarian dictatorship. Russia today is an authoritarian dictatorship and China's Communist Party is well on the way to creating one there. North Korea fits this model. In the world today there are about eight totalitarian dictatorships and perhaps another dozen countries leaning toward becoming one.

In America, especially in the South, there was a real fear of creating a government with the power to control and interfere in the operations of the individual citizens, commerce, local government, and the states. As had been practiced in the series of semi-formal Congresses leading up to the Declaration of Independence and during the Revolutionary War, the country was governed by people sent to the Congress by the states. They voted amongst themselves democratically for the war, the peace, and the formation of a Federal Government. They generally were not elected, but rather were appointed by the governments of the colonies or by groups who were challenging British appointed governors.

Many of the leaders in the northeast were among the most educated and offered well-reasoned ideas for that government. In a way they were what some today might refer to as an educated elite, which, after the experiences of living in a monarchy, felt enlightened enough to guide the formation of the new nation. (The political system used in those early congresses and in the first few years after the Revolutionary War was a Representative Democracy. The people elected state governments who in turn appointed members of congress.)

Others, many from the South and less populated states away from New England, were more individual liberty and opportunity focused. Equally educated, they were fewer in number. While they had often lost fewer citizens in the war than the New England states, they had paid a terrible price in percentage of dead and wounded and economic devastation. They were concerned about creating a strong national leader, and also the tyranny of a majority. That is, they were concerned that large population states could dominate the smaller states just because they had more people. All of the representatives desired a representative democracy, where the best of each state would be elected and sent to represent the state in the congresses of the future. The question was, how did they balance large state populations and policies with the different interests of smaller states. How did they balance rural agricultural interest with industrial?

The first national agreement, THE ARTICLES OF CONFEDERATION were so weak that there was almost no central government and little cooperation among the states. The failures of the ARTICLES OF CONFEDERATION became apparent in five years.

THE CONSTITUTION AND LEGISLATION

As with everything from the Declaration of Independence on, the founders arrived at a compromise; a **constitutional republic that elected representatives democratically.** The Constitution of the

United States was created seven years after the war ended to **limit the political power of the majority and government.** It specifically limits the power of those who are elected to office. Members of the House of Representatives would be allocated based on population, favoring the large states. Members of the Senate would be allocated two per state balancing the power of large states. A court system would settle disagreements and enforce national laws. The founding fathers all saw the Federal Government as doing only those functions that the people first and then the states could not accomplish or where collectively through the new Federal Government, they could be more efficient and economical.

Ben Franklin once spoke to the power of liberty in a Constitutional Democracy, "Democracy is two wolves and a lamb voting on what to have for lunch. Liberty is a well-armed lamb contesting the vote."

The Constitution is the primary code of law in the nation. It finally brought the founding states together into an organized nation. It is very narrow and very specific, and all other laws created in the nation, whether local, state, or national must not run afoul of the Constitution. It allocates very specific responsibilities to the national government. Article 1, section 8 assigns only about 18 responsibilities to the Federal Government. The Constitution specifically reserves all others to the people or the states. Judges must look at every case, whether civil or criminal and apply the appropriate laws created by elected officials, but only after determining whether that law is allowed under the Constitution. A Constitution gives the country a **set of principles** and guides all other governmental decisions. It recognizes that society may evolve and provides for a method to amend the Constitution, something that has happened 27 times but to avoid changes driven by societal issues of the day, that change can only happen if the majority of the states agree to the change. That Constitution guarantees the rights of ordinary citizens to work and create wealth and security for their families. Further, it guarantees the rights of those citizens to band together to create business to harness the power of the group to create wealth. It envisions those citizens creating governments that do only what they cannot do themselves. It protects personal freedoms, speech, religion, self-defense, the ability to organize, halt illegal search and seizure, and so on, from any form of government interference. In America, you actually have a legal right to differ from the government or the majority, even to be wrong.

The Constitution, along with the amendments is about 41 pages long, small, narrow, and concise. In comparison, our Federal Government has become bloated, gangly, and inefficient. Think about the comparison of the founding Constitution as amended over the last 240 years and the most recent Federal budget bill; 41 pages versus 2700 pages. Have you ever tried to do more than you can efficiently accomplish? That is the Federal Government today, and it shows in all of our lives. Government's failure to fix problems, frustrates all of us. (Today the airline industry is cancelling flights because it is terribly short on pilots, while the FAA fumbles through approving many pilot medicals, with a backlog of a years of reviews. In the case of a pilot who has surrendered their medical certificate in order to receive medical treatment or where a pilot has lost their certificate due to other issues, the FAA certifies private medical doctors to help these pilots return to service. Then they refuse to listen to those doctors and refer every case to a FAA doctor for final approval. But there are only a handful of FAA employed doctors, so nothing happens and there is no plan to fix the problem.) The bureaucrats refuse to listen to the doctors they certified to conduct pilot medicals.

What the Constitution does not allow is for citizens, lawmakers, or judges to make decisions purely based on what they believe or want. The majority belief today may not be the majority belief in the future and in any event, those beliefs do not necessarily hold sway over others who believe differently. If you think about it, the vast majority of Americans in 1789 when the Constitution was adopted had spent their entire life with slavery of other human beings as an accepted right. There were 31,000,000 citizens, and 4,000,000 slaves. A vocal minority of citizens opposed slavery and in spite of being outnumbered by perhaps four to one, slavery was among the first issues that congress dealt with. In 50 years, in a dozen increments, slavery was outlawed in America. Could it have been done faster? Maybe, but not even the most strident abolitionists could define an alternative that would keep the economy working. (Interestingly, the abolition of slavery drove technological revolutions that within decades replaced much of the work formerly done by slaves with machines. Within a century those machines have created a controversy of their own as the nation has become concerned about the pollution they create. Other machines continue to replace workers, and history has taught us that loss of jobs from productive new technology is inevitable and that most of those productive improvements yield a higher standard of living for all. It has also taught us that a flexible, well-educated work force must be ready to move into newly created opportunities.

There is no provision in the Constitution for diversity, equity, and inclusion. Inclusion and diversity are social arguments, and the Constitution does not allow or disallow either. When the Constitution was created America was already a diverse nation. One example of that reality was that when the Constitution was approved, and population calculations for electing members of Congress were adopted, every slave counted as 2/3 of a person for census. From day one, the country saw slaves as human, just not as human as non-slaves. You can scream that this was unfair and judge America for taking five decades to outlaw slavery or you can rejoice in the fact that after 4,000 years it was rejected in half a century. You have a right to either opinion.

Inclusion, if it is part of an effort to assure the rights of all, is allowed. The voting rights act of 1965 helped raise black registered voters in much of the South from about 8% to comparable to whites today. Equity is a bit more complicated. The founding documents of the country speak to equal opportunity for all, not equal outcome. The Constitution and Bill of Rights, added by amendment, emphasize the rights of the individual and they are not to be interfered with by the majority or government. Under the American Constitution, you have the right to earn a vast fortune or to fail. The founding fathers saw poverty as a temporary state, something that churches or other civil institutions would address and felt confident that the nation's citizens would never allow themselves to become parasites on the economy; they would get off the dole as quickly as possible and work to prove those who helped them were justified in their efforts. We believe that is still the case in America, but the actions and policies of government have severely damaged the sense of liberty, independence, and initiative that the founding fathers believed in.

Over the years, vocal minorities have pushed through laws that are intended to reduce or eliminate inequity and promote social and environmental justice. As long as these laws do not interfere with the guaranteed right under the Constitution, generally they have been allowed. Some, like Women's Suffrage were critical successes. A policy argument supports them while, in some cases a legal constitutional examination does not. By that I mean, in the name of greater equity we constrain the liberty of some, constrain their beliefs and behavior and reallocate their wealth. Often these laws make it more difficult to achieve and accumulate wealth or worse, punish the entire economy. Historically, many of the most trumpeted new legal policies struggle to meet their goals. All too often the groups developing these policies and laws are single issue organizations with great expertise in one specific area, (hydrocarbon impact on warming for example), but little understanding of the targeted industries, their customers, or their operational place in the economy. They ignore the impact of the policies on world order. Inevitably many of these legal policies hurt some while trying to help others. And the promoters of the new policies smile and tell us that is okay, even desirable.

A critical example of this was the recent policy that regulated away America's energy independence by closing oil exploration on public lands, keeping newly developed sources from production, and shutting down pipelines. The intent was to make fossil fuel more expensive, driving down demand. With higher fossil energy costs, expensive 'clean' alternatives would supposedly become more attractive.

The problem was there was nothing yet available to replace the lost fossil fuel production and demand continued. Within months energy costs in the U.S. doubled and the President literally begged Saudi Arabia and Russia to increase fuel production. Inflation soared, discretionary income disappeared for many families, and there was no increase in alternative energy production. Energy became a weapon in the hands of a Russian dictator, and he began blackmailing the western world. While energy costs in the U.S. doubled, in Europe they tripled and Russia which produces 30% of the energy used in Europe threatened to leave Europe cold and in the dark. Convinced that nobody dare challenge him, the Russian president launched the first large scale war in Europe in 75 years. Once again that law of unintended consequences. No matter how deeply you believe in attacking global warming by curtailing American fossil fuel production, you by now can see the costs of this policy. The poor in this country are poorer, the middle class struggling, Ukrainians are dying by the thousands, and the pollution from thousands of burning buildings, fuels storage areas and vehicles is adding enormous pollution to the air.

(The goals of slowing the impact of man on the environment are worthy but cutting fuel sources before there was a working alternative turned out to be a lot like cutting well water flow to a city before the new plant to pull water from a river was working.

It seems like a good idea until you cannot get your child a glass of water.) Every one of us is suffering and at real risk from conflict. The economy, shaken by what is happening is not favorable for wealth creation and entrepreneurial innovation. The stock market is contracting which, if you are one of those who feel the wealthy do not deserve the money they earned, I guess is good. But virtually every retirement plan in the country is also contracting. Those already drawing retirement are cutting where they can, and others will find that they must postpone retirement until the markets recover. Fewer employees are moving up the ladder, and those that are find that their higher pay is being canceled by run-away inflation. Those at the bottom of the economic ladder are hurt the most. If they can find entry level work the opportunity to move up is curtailed. The tendency is to pass laws to tax those who are working to help those who are not, drawing even more money from the capital pool used to start new business and expand successful ones.

We do not argue that government cannot enact these types of policies. Because of the steady expansion of federal power and authority, and where judges believe that policy and legal precedent are equal, government is doing that. But by Natural Law and careful constitutional evaluation, they are troublesome. What is not questionable is damage done by emotionally charged law making, that is narrowly tailored to solve one problem without taking into account the unintended consequences that hurt us all.

The nation is terribly torn by the reversal of Roe v. Wade. At one point to promote popular policy, the Court held that all women had a constitutional right to an abortion by stretching the 14th amendment language way outside what was actually in the amendment, only to change that decision fifty years later. The new decision found that the Courts really had no constitutional role in abortion and maybe not the Federal Government at all. That is a policy issue and as such reserved to the people and the legislatures of the states. Since its creation, the Supreme Court has overturned

300 of its own decisions, on subjects as diverse as Child Labor, Separate but Equal treatment of education, citizenship restrictions, Federal vs State supremacy, Free Speech, Issues of incrimination, issues of discrimination, and justice and due process under the law. One case on Admiralty law issues was overturned after 136 years; another, a search and seizure decision made in 1982 was overturned in 1983. In most of these cases, a future court reprimanded and reversed an earlier court who had stretched the role of the courts and the Federal Government to support what was at the time popular policy. In most of those reversals, the congress or state legislators then took on the issues, (sometimes over a period of time), and enacted legislation that set the policies into law, decided that the policy needed to be changed, or more often, arrived at some form of compromise that spoke to all sides of the issue. The Dobbs decision did not make abortion illegal in America, but it did make clear that the federal courts had no say in a decision that belongs to the people and their elected legislative representatives. Those who feel strongly on the issue, on either side, have the greatest reason to talk to those they disagree with to reach a solution. The justice's job is to listen to the argument, look at the evidence and make a hard decision, based on the Constitution, not policy.

The nation now has alternatives available on abortion, where in the 1970's the only two options were safe medical procedures or what used to be called 'coat-hanger abortion' a too often deadly option. The real social impact of the Dobbs decision will be known within a few years. Few believe, even those who are passionate about ending abortion, that abortion will be totally illegal. (Abortion on a per-capita basis is already dramatically lower than in the 1970's. The issue is being diminished by better birth control access and a substantial shift in the public's beliefs.)

(I believe that the nation would be better served if the limitations of the Constitution and legal argument remain superior to policy. That would force our leaders to carefully tailor policy instead of responding to the loudest voices and would ensure a more careful evaluation of the laws of unintended consequences. As I rewrite this section, the President is desperately trying to 'MODIFY' his energy policy without totally infuriating the environmental wing of his party. The United States production of natural gas is the only viable alternative to Russian natural gas in Europe. It is the viable counter to Putin's mindset, "Let the bastards freeze to death in the dark.)

What is the impact on you? Perhaps none if you live off the grid and grow your own food and walk everywhere. But I hope it leads many who embrace strong beliefs in a better society to ignore sloganeering and really dig deeper into the political decisions and contributions they make. There is no reduction in energy demand despite driving up fossil fuel cost. How do we save the world by giving a mad man dictator a tool that convinces him that he can start a war and then threaten any nation who interferes with nuclear attack? If history has taught us anything, it's that miscalculations are part of every war and in a world with nuclear weapons it would only take one miscalculation to made environmental change irrelevant.

Even the pollution justification argument is questionable. Some in the Biden administration wanted to show off their commitment to the American environmental movement by crippling American energy production. Importing foreign oil requires transport by oil tanker. It takes an average of five days from onloading a tanker to the arrival at a receiving port. It takes the same average of five days for that tanker to return for the next load. It takes a day to load a tanker and two to unload one. In this environment of clogged American ports, the average wait time to unload is four days. The average tanker burns 2,600 gallons of fuel per hour at sea and perhaps half of that at rest. That means that one delivery of fuel, taking a tanker 17 days will dump the pollution from 842,000 gallons of fuel oil into the atmosphere. Some estimates for CO2 emissions run as high as 27 million tons per trip. I would love to see any data that might prove that this is superior to North American produced oil moved by pipeline.

Much of the legal collision between what the media calls strict constitutional jurists and more liberal judges began in the early 1900's with the election of Woodrow Wilson to the presidency. Wilson was a self-declared progressive who pushed through a very aggressive list of bills to assert the power of the Federal Government over industry and the states. These included such important laws as child labor laws and the creation of the Federal Reserve. It also included several bills that tore responsibilities from the states and redeposited them with the Federal Government. Wilson saw the nation as one big pot of similar if not identical culture, and the Federal Government as the policeman assuring that everyone did what they were told. The problem was that Wilson and his tiny group of advisors failed to see the differences across the land and picked winners and losers. Much of his decision making was based on the color of people's skin.

Many of the bills he pushed through Congress were questionable under the Constitution, but Wilson as former president of Princeton University, Governor of New Jersey, and the only president who had a PhD, aggressively pushed judges, especially those who he appointed to reinterpret the Constitution to allow legislation that addressed what he believed were critical societal needs. From that time on, groups like the current liberal legal think tank, **Demand Justice** have argued that policy is just as critical as law. They argue that broad interpretation of the intentions and goals, not just the actual words of the Constitution, should be the basis of legal opinion.

As noted before, one of the critical responsibilities of the Constitution is to lay out a set of **principles** that guide the law and society. It also is supposed to protect against tyranny of either the majority or minority. Opening the words and intent of the Constitution to whatever interpretation elected officials find expedient takes away that principled guidance. President Wilson, the father of American Progressivism, was for example, a blatant anti-black racist. He used liberal legal interpretation, based on policy, to roll back most of the laws and rules of the reconstruction period; rules that opened the doors and offered opportunity to former slaves and their offspring. He went so far as honoring the Ku Klux Klan as he moved to repeal the anti-Klan legislation passed after the Civil War. The result was an almost total removal of black employees from the Federal Government and pressure for other government, social and business groups to do the same. Wilson saw black people as vastly inferior and saw it as his duty to keep them away from the enlightened white people who elected him.

If Wilson really believed that the nation's primary codified law, the Constitution, needed revision, he had the amendment process available to him. But that takes years, and approval by the states, so it was more expedient to promote judges who think their beliefs allow them to reinterpret that document. Wilson, representing what he believed was a majority, almost single handedly demolished fifty years of social and economic justice for families of former slaves. He encouraged local anti-black activity from groups like the KKK. Other people of color were also singled out. I doubt that Wilson wanted to see them starve, but he surely did not want Black American participation in government or the economy. (This was in line with the Southern Democratic (Dixiecrat) policies followed since reconstruction. Black America's place in the economy was to provide menial labor.)

As a progressive, Wilson also supported the Bolshevik Revolution in Russia. The new Communist government then betrayed his support by backing out of the war against Germany in World War I, collapsing the Eastern Front just as American troops were taking over the majority of fighting on the Western Front. The unintended consequences of his support of the Bolsheviks cost the lives of thousands of American servicemen. The egalitarian utopia

Wilson expected in Russia was instead twisted to death by leaders, turned authoritarian, Lenin and later Joseph Stalin. These enlightened leaders squashed all dissent in the name of equity.

Overly broad legal interpretations led to judicial decisions with substantial social impact. Wilson championed the idea that policy was equal to the Constitution in the courts. Many socially driven legal decisions were overturned in the future, after years of suffering by those impacted. (In 2022 the Supreme Court finally addressed the separation of church and state issues in the Constitution. Progressive thinkers promoting the traditional idea of public education have for decades made it illegal for government funds to go to religious schools. Even voucher programs provided to parents for educational support could not go to religious schools. Yet in many communities the best schools were religious based and the only people who could afford them were upper income Americans. Minority parents and students were left out. But in the 2022 decision, the Supreme Court ruled that separation of Church and State was valid but <u>could not discriminate</u> against any school just because it was faith based. This opens the doors of some of America's best schools to people who could not otherwise afford them and raises the bar for the performance of all schools.)

Since Wilson's term, other American presidents have followed his model with the same consequences. Wilson's willingness to defy the Constitution set back the advancement of former slaves in the American economy like nothing else. It legitimized racism in political decision making. It also laid the groundwork for the courts and legislatures imposing huge burdens on individual citizens working to create wealth for their families and personal liberty. As President, he set in place laws and policies arguing that a minority of the nation's citizens didn't have a real right to the American dream because they looked different and obviously were inferior.

The conservative compass has not changed. It is focused on liberty and the freedom of individual citizens to create wealth, participate in groups dedicated to improving the economic well-being of the members, and an insistence that government has no right to interfere with those pursuits. Most emphasize that Natural Americans do not have the right to hurt other Americans. Like the Democrats, the Republicans have some members who twist policy to fit personal prejudices, but those members on each side are a small minority. Republicans historically only support what they view as constitutional legislation that focuses on liberty and individual rights within a limited government, they generally do not support legal schemes that take from one to give to another. Today the Republican Party has become a populist party, not the internationalist economic driven party of the last century. Still, the party platform has changed little. But few from either party, can look at **any person or family** that is struggling without being concerned. Personal feelings, our emotional response, encourages us to help. Conservative thoughts on help always center on creating opportunity for people to go as far as they can. Many of our friends on the left look at unwillingness to embrace legislative policies that transfer resources, (wealth) to help the less fortunate and see libertarians and conservatives as uncaring. Some are, but the majority are unwilling to pay people to tread water, to abandon the dream to really succeed.

WHAT IS THE DIFFERENCE BETWEEN 'ACTIONS BASED ON THINKING' VERSUS 'ACTIONS BASED ON FEELING'?

Melody, you answered the last question on the survey as follows:

"Thinking actions would be based on facts, but only as gained from reliable sources. Feeling actions often are based on our personal experiences and may be objective or biased. Often decisions based on feelings lead us to jump to conclusions or are just emotional responses. You need to think before you act."

People like the author are not non-emotional, unconcerned idiots. We believe that trying to solve societal problems by enlisting government, from a purely emotional foundation, creates more problems than it solves. You may well accomplish more by putting your thinking and emotions together and tackle the issues yourself or with like-minded citizens on your own.

At the same time, conservatives emphasize citizen rights to life, liberty, and **the Pursuit** of happiness. They champion individual rights, opportunity, and responsibility without government interference. When civil society struggles to overcome problems, as in the great depression or voting rights in the South in the first half of the 20th Century, government can help, but that help should be short lived. Once the problem is diminished, or if government's role isn't helping, it should end. Conservatives believe that many government programs have resulted in citizens being paid to sit on the bench instead of playing the game. Is the conservative idea of free access to the political world and economy enough to eliminate social inequity? Who knows, because government has intervened in the process constantly since the 1960's. (Remember that the author is a registered independent. In spite of the rhetoric, few citizens blame any one party for the nation's woes, rather we are concerned that decisions based on feelings rather than thinking often hurt more than they help. Both parties have replaced a lot of thinking with a lot of emotion. Neither side is listening to the other.)

History shows us that the Democratic party spent 100 years trying to protect a racially driven belief that lesser human beings needed to be kept in their place. When it became obvious that the nation was moving from that repression, they switched tactics. Instead of battling the Republicans determined to assure the constitutional rights of all, they accepted the inevitable with support for the Civil Rights acts of the mid 1960's. What were planned as short-term bridge social benefit programs to assist the less fortunate never went away. Instead, as economic reform led to the rust belt, the Democrats doubled down on these benefit plans. The results are clear, the laws and policies passed have paid a large segment of the population not to fully participate in the most vibrant economy on earth. It has shortchanged those people and the economy by robbing it of workers and innovators. It has created pockets of economic suffering and then offered to buy the people ramen and spam. The media then looks at those same people and asks, why doesn't the government provide steak and fresh vegetables? It has encouraged even school systems and teachers to protect their share of the dream by opposing meaningful reform, leaving tens of thousands of students woefully short on the skills to fully participate in the economy. Most teachers know it can be better. We all should be incensed.

The media and literally hundreds of organizations who profess to fight for the rights of the less fortunate begin every effort by telling the very people they want to help that they are victims, that the SYSTEM is keeping them from succeeding. We acknowledge that some groups of Americans have developed emotional trauma. We do not argue that there are significant obstacles from full participation in the economy, there are. But while these barriers, mostly created by government are dismantled, one at a time, what is accomplished by telling people that they cannot jump over them on their own? How does it help to tell the less fortunate that since they can't get ahead on their own, the government will pay them a little more not to participate?

(What I do not agree with is hysterical emotional screaming about our history. To those who did not experience slavery or were not old enough to participate in the Civil Rights movement of the 1960's and 1970's, emotional responses to what people experienced is not helping any of those who were there. History is not for any of us to like or dislike, it is there for us to learn from. If you study the history, not the slogans, you will see progress. You will see that many who participated in things we disagree with, like owning slaves, also did remarkable things that make our lives richer and more successful. Few in history had no flaws.)

Across the American Midwest and West, in the farming and ranching belt, there are hundreds of ghost towns that became obsolete as the agricultural economy changed. The Federal Government's creation of the National Highway system also made it easy to bypass small towns to shop in larger communities with more variety. Government did nothing to save failing towns. Yet in the withering cities of the rust belt, government clings to a belief that the economic laws do not apply. Water and sewer systems erode. Road maintenance disintegrates. Hospitals close making health care more difficult. Again, worst of all, poor education systems evolve to explain away poor academic performance by pointing to the difficult lives of parents and students. With little local economic opportunity, those students who do well, move away creating a brain drain. Eroding tax bases force government to press the remaining businesses and industries for more help, cutting profits and making reinvestment to aging infrastructure difficult. Many businesses close or move to a new, more business-friendly location. More jobs are lost.

So, Melody, what do we do to change the trajectory of the nation? **First, we demand educational performance.** This does not mean abandoning failing public schools, but it does mean unleashing the power of the thousands of educators and parents who realize that what worked in the 1950's is not working in the 2020's. Whether it be charter schools or financial support for highly motivated student to go to private schools, the first thing we need to break down is the comradery of victimhood and the fear to move out of the pack, to risk reaching for excellence. Public teachers' unions are filled with capable, competent teachers, but not all. There are a lot of teachers who are not willing to buck the system. The steady paycheck and benefits are critical to teachers. Teachers are critical to students. Still, what about union leaders who ask teachers annually to give money to politicians who do not have the will to make real fundamental improvements? In fact, they solicit money to keep politicians in office just so they will not make any changes. Many unions and the politicians they favor thrive on continued educational inefficiency. How often have we all heard, 'with just a little more government funding ...' With that said, something different needs to be done. The public is not willing to pay more to prop up poor educational performance. Until reading, writing, arithmetic, social studies, (civics) and history skills improve, the public will have a very limited appetite for more educational taxes or spending.

I'm not talking about the historical rote learning memorization technique. At a recent holiday get-together, my grandson was proud to show off his knowledge of how the Articles of Confederation was replaced by the Constitution. That is great to know, important. What was missing from the narrative was the educational system challenging him to discuss why that Constitution is important and how. It is missing the thinking part of 'what this means to me is.'

The social indoctrination of kids is not helping. Reinforcing to needy kids that they are victims does not create a clear message that they can win, even if it requires beating the system. Telling kids that are more well to do, that they are oppressors does not launch them into the kind of hard work and innovation that will lead them to create business, grow wealth, give others an opportunity through employment and innovation. Teaching fear and inequity to one group and superiority and shame to the other accomplishes what? One message that all students need to hear is that they can win, not just participate. Get rid of the participation trophy mindset. Let those who are not succeeding learn that failure is an important part of learning to succeed. Standing at the plate and striking out, should only teach us that we need to work on our hitting. Failing at anything hurts, but it is also a great motivator to do better. A second message is that the pie needs to be bigger for all. Everyone can help achieve that. Hearing high school kids tell you that there's not much need to really perform, to prepare for the future because global warming is going to kill us all anyway should scare the hell out of us.

One of the great examples of success is my friend John. He was from East St. Louis and grew up with a mom who was a nurse's aide. He lost his father at a young age. His stepfather worked in Civil Service. Combined the family never made twenty-five thousand dollars in a year. Not much to support a family of seven. The neighborhood is the poorest in America, almost all black, and filled with examples of failure. People there 'just don't have a chance.'

His parents struggled to overcome community influences with their faith-based messages.

John refused to be sucked in. He did a work study program at his high school, qualifying by entrance exam. Only 15% of the mixed-race pool of applicants were admitted to the program. His job, working around blue collar workers and management in an auto parts company showed him success. Entry workers who worked hard and intelligently moved up. Those same workers encouraged him to be something. He watched how they managed their lives and looked to the future. He took the $700 he had saved and applied to a State University. His stepfather told him he was nuts, that he was wasting his money. He used some grant money and continued working to graduate. Nothing was going to stop him, nothing did.

Next, he joined the Air Force as an intelligence officer and later was a successful sales manager for a national life insurance company. At every step people discussed obstacles and at every step John saw only the next opportunity. He still sees only the next opportunity. Not all of his siblings have been as successful. John saw only hurdles to jump over. Others spent their early years stymied by perceived obstacles.

The second thing we do to change the trajectory of the

nation is take all of the rusting infrastructure and abandoned real estate and invite business to put it to work. Tear down the barriers, including tax and environmental barriers. If a clean-up is needed, government can help, even if zealots call this corporate welfare. After all, the environmental community is deeply entrenched in government. Realize that some jobs are entry level and are most valuable just because they give new workers an opportunity to learn work habits and skills. But even here, business cannot locate to sites where they cannot find educated, prepared workers. They are reluctant to open shop in areas under siege from crime and violence. We need to make manufacturing a critical part of our economy again. We need to help communities overcome the violence that tears at people's souls.

Pay attention to the regulatory climate in your community and recognize that a lot of regulation on the books and proposed regulation does not accomplish its goals and interferes with business development. For example, in real estate development, it has become fashionable to demand developers invest millions of dollars in community infrastructure in order to get permits to proceed on new housing. New roads and local road upgrades may be required. A land set aside for new parks and school sites may be required. Utility companies can request huge upgrades to their networks, upgrades that often are not needed, but cover the utility for doing upgrade maintenance that they have ignored for years. In the end, the developer, who in good faith had planned a mixed income development cannot make the project work without dedicating most of the project to upper income homes. But the local government folks still trumpet the huge success of creating more housing knowing full well that the real housing crisis is to house lower income citizens. Look at our nice new school. A school that is located miles from where one was needed. So now we need more tax money to buy more busses and hire drivers.

Next, we have to remove the stigma from starting at the bottom that has become prevalent in society. As noted early in the book, I love Black History Month. It is sad that there has to be a separate month to recognize the contribution of America's Black Citizens, but anything that counterbalances the constant drumbeat of victimhood is critical. Honestly, as a kid, we learned as much about George Washington Carver as Thomas Edison. One of the failures of public education is that it does not <u>honor the creators</u> in our economy, creators of any heritage.

Clearly most of the inventors featured in history and the news have been white, but not all. (There were, on average, eight times more white Americans than black, and until the late 1800's few black Americans were climbing the economic ladder.) Personal pride fuels confidence which in turn makes risk taking acceptable. The fastest way to fail is not to try even if that attempt is a startup job or in an environment that makes you uncomfortable. To be a bit uncomfortable is to many a little unreasonable, but remember all progress is dependent on unreasonable people. Personal progress is often dependent on leaps of faith.

As President Teddy Roosevelt used to say, "Do what you can with what you have, wherever you are."

Your personal beliefs may open way more stairways to success than we note here. The challenge is to make them focused on the success of all, in the future, without constant focus on them versus us.

I learned that Black Americans fought in the Revolutionary War (for both sides), the War of 1812 (for both sides), The Civil War (for both sides), the Spanish American War, World War I, World War II, and Korea. We're old enough to know several who have fought in subsequent wars. We were not taught about the Medal of Honor winners of any race in any war with the exception of Sergeant York in WW-I and Audie Murphy in WW-II. How sad. One of the blogs I follow is dedicated to heroes of the military and in those posts have learned about Medal of Honor winners of almost every race in America. Did many face hurdles and struggles beyond their fellow soldiers, airmen and sailors? Yes. Did their service, especially in WW-II lay the groundwork for far greater integration into the American economy? Yes. Among my personal heroes were the Nisei Japanese American soldiers of the 442 regimental combat team who fought in Europe and the Red-Tailed Devils (the Tuskegee Airmen) an extraordinary group of fighter pilots. One group were Japanese Americans and the other Black Americans. Honestly, I cannot recall the designation of any other units who fought in Europe. But we do recall the incredible success of the Navajo Code Talkers, who used their native language to confuse the Japanese military. In my fiction book, ENEMY PATRIOTS, I focused on how critical Japanese Americans were to MIS field intelligence that helped win WW-II. Few know they even existed.

One of the Rat Pack, the performer Sammy Davis Jr, was a black army officer in WW-II. Arriving home in the deep south, in uniform, he boarded a city bus and was told to 'move to the back of the bus.'

"I'm not black," said Sammy, "I'm Jewish."

"Well then son, you will have to get off from my bus," he was told.

But it never slowed him down. He just roared onto the scene as a talented performer and made his fortune. He was respected and beloved.

Pride in who and what you are is important to success. Learning about Natural Americans who served, helped not hurt other Americans, took on extraordinary responsibility, and built great wealth works for all of us. In one way or another almost every famous black person has spoken to how their spirit was crushed little by little, and then they overcame. Nothing will remedy trauma like personal and family success for every citizen. I just wish that we could discard the hyphenated prefix. The continual drumbeat of division does nothing for anyone.

LOCAL LAW ENFORCEMENT

I don't know that I ever heard more comments of total disgust than those about the murder of George Floyd. The guy had a long criminal record but that does not excuse his murder. The uproar was all justified. No Natural American has the right to harm another, and that is especially true of one sworn to protect and serve.

The recent police shootings of a half-dozen other people of color have ripped at this nation. The judicial system has, over the years, favored the blue people over those of every other color. I can't justify that but as one former cop explained more than a decade ago, "Especially in high crime environments, you go out every day and put your life on the line. You make life and death decisions in seconds. You feel your life and livelihood may be at risk every time you respond to a call; nobody likes this. There are some places where we know we are at greater risk than others, and we can't ignore that." The Blue Wall is infamous. Ask yourself if the hundreds of millions of dollars in social spending has reduced or induced violence in America. Now ask yourself if clearly offering those struggling economically a clear vision of what it takes to be a Natural American, free to succeed might do.

So, where is the solution? I really don't know but believe that it starts with every citizen taking responsibility for their own personal behavior. People who take what is not there's or create wealth with minimal effort by selling drugs or robbing their neighbors are not taking responsibility for their own behavior. Before we discuss police actions and statistical information about police actions and racism, lets first recognize that the real victims of crime are those who are wronged. The robbery, assault, sexual violence, domestic violence, embezzlement, hate crime, murder and other criminal offenses always leave a victim of the crime distraught, injured, or dead. These are all people, or families, who will need support to recover. Someone stole part or all of their life, their wealth, their time. People of color suffer way too high a proportion.

Nobody has a right to create wealth by taking it illegally from another. Nobody has the right to harm another citizen. There is no social justification for criminal behavior. The police performance overall in America seems well focused on these facts. I personally believe that some of the training that various police departments have embraced in the last 20 years has created a culture where assisting victims is not enough, the policemen feel a need to punish. Much of this training evolved from the militarization of police efforts such as SWAT. I've personally interacted with cops who are compensating for prior lives of being left out or ignored, by becoming bullies. With that said, the actual number of illegal or morally corrupt police actions is miniscule. Black families have what they call, 'the talk' especially with their sons. They emphasize that police encounters can be dangerous and teach their kids to be careful with their speech and actions around cops. This used to be called common courtesy and respect for authority. It is more important to black men than white men but works for all men.

What is not miniscule is the crime in America. For many it is easier to create wealth by taking advantage of other citizens. The uniform crime reporting program noted the following. In 2020, 69% of all those arrested were white, 27% were black and 4% other races. That year, approximately 62% of the population was white, 12% black and 26% other races. Overall, white and black Americans appear to dominate the activities of police departments.

If you look at the most brutal crime, homicide, the numbers are really warped. In 2019, 16% of whites were killed by other whites, 3% of white people were killed by police, and 81% were killed by black people. That same year, 2% of black fatalities came from whites killing blacks, 1% were police killing blacks, and 97% were black citizens killing other black citizens.

I make this point for two reasons. First, while there are blatant examples of police treating different races differently, statistically police actions are fairly even. Second, the amount of black-on-black crime is out of control. The number of police encounters with violent black citizens is way out of proportion to the percentage of black citizens. Police fatal shootings would appear to be skewed in that 27% of the shootings were of black people who represent only 13% of the population. But the percentage of police violent crime encounters with black suspects is more than three times their percentage of the general population. Why is this important, because whatever government has been investing to support our black citizens is failing us and them. Among the most important parts of being a Natural American is to honor and take care of fellow Americans. Overall violence in many inner cities is crushing people's ability to make their lives better, to create wealth. It is justification for trauma, and it needs to stop.

Pointing to some economic or social issues is valid. So is the simple reality that irresponsible, illegal, and violent behavior of some who have never had or lost their moral compass is epidemic. If you were a cop on the beat in many cities in America, encountering potential lethal encounters with black citizens is way out of proportion to their percentage of the population. This does not justify a quick decision to use lethal force, but conditioning from regular dangerous situations is human nature. This is where enhanced risk management training may help for police. Clear education on how our Constitutional Democracy is supposed to work and how to be a full player in the economy could work for all citizens. We need to teach, **you own you.**

In violent encounters, and homicide, the answer will come from churches, social support groups and more, not less police presence. Once a case goes to trial, it is clear that personal economic strength helps in the American courts. People with money are more successful in evading responsibility for criminal acts. Some laws like the insane laws that punish crack users far more harshly than cocaine users need to go. Sentencing needs to fit the crime. But criminals need to be sentenced, not released. And perhaps most importantly, incarceration needs to be remedial and the stigma of incarceration which keeps people who have done their time from employment needs fixing. Some of what is needed is government's role, but most is up to us. Let's cut criminal behavior and encourage all citizens to become Natural Americans with the resources to balance financial advantage in the courts.

But what does not make a lot of sense is to excuse violent criminal behavior; to ignore sentencing from valid trials because of someone's color. There is no color code on a moral compass.

Simply unleashing the power of the economy and preparing people to create wealth legally will solve a lot of the crime; that and people taking responsibility for their own behavior. We understand the concerns of movements like Black Lives Matter but will always extend more empathy for the victims of crime than the perpetrators and believe that the vast majority of Americans of all colors agree. The loss of life in a shootout with a drug dealer is sad, but the loss of life of a child caught up in a gang shootout is tragic. Over the years I've employed people who had been incarcerated. Their reformed moral and social commitment to create honest wealth and help their fellow man made them really good employees. I have also fired and prosecuted others who forgot their personal responsibility.

The behavior of primarily spoiled white kids in places like Portland and Seattle has no place in society. Allowing such riotous behavior to destroy communities because the participants feel bad is a stunning failure of society. It is also a stunning critique of the failure of many parents to teach about the 'great responsibility' requirement of being a Natural American.

Much of the problem lies with how we as a nation have decided to tackle social and economic problems. Our tendency, to look to the federal government to remedy social ills inevitably means that bureaucrats, most in Washington DC, decide what will work and suck up half of the tax revenues collected to help with paperwork and inefficiency. What if we made it very attractive for Natural Americans to support local groups who are closer to and more knowledgeable of the problems? Can you imagine how much good organizations driven by, for example, black churches or youth programs could do with the money? (We speak here of the black churches committed to promoting liberty, responsibility, and success among their parishioners, not those who preach division and victimhood. A black friend told me recently that the fastest way to get your house burned down is to challenge the doctrine of a victim oriented black church. Poverty is big business.) Those closer to the people could really target help to those who were already committed to making their and their family's lives better. A real awareness of those who looked back at past mistakes with a commitment to improve themselves, their families and their community can't hurt. Problems are better solved by people close to the problem.

"There is nothing noble in being superior to your fellow man. True nobility lies in being superior to your former self." (Ernest Hemingway)

You own you and only you are responsible to your fellow man.

Okay, I will quietly pour another cup of coffee, and if it will not offend you Melody, I wish I could refill your cup as well. If we were walking into a coffee shop, I would probably hold the door for you, not because you cannot do that yourself, but because that is what I was taught since childhood. I do not challenge what you see as the truth. I am comfortable that one form of truth is based on hard science, observable and recognized by anyone who tests it. I also realize that the other form of truth is based on our beliefs, dependent on facts that not all of us share or even interpret the same way. Still, to you and to us they are truth.

Much of this book is dedicated to sharing with you the economic, historic, legal, and societal beliefs that make up what I call truth. Your interpretation of the same components is every bit as valid to your truths. And while I hope to have exposed you to some different beliefs, some different historical facts, what we hope for the most is that you can see that what I want in America is similar to what you want.

If that is the case, then we need to quit screaming at each other and calling each other names. Angry social media posts just fuel division and assure that we talk at each other instead of with each other. How is it helping us to allow media moguls and their employees to grow rich by trumpeting division and discord? Both sides are growing wealthy by pitting us against one another. Remember we set out to have a discussion, not a debate.

Perhaps even after reading this book, you feel that the entire idea of the Natural American and the work ethic and results of that definition do not fit your narrative. Perhaps you feel that you are entitled to wealth and well-being just because you exist, and that the only thing you owe some fellow citizens is to scream at the top of your lungs that they too are entitled. Well, I tried and did not get the conversation started that I hoped for. If this is you, you don't need to finish this book. But thank you for your time and consideration.

If on the other hand, we can agree on the personal responsibility part of creating wealth with as little work as possible and doing it in an honorable way that helps, not harms your fellow American, then read on. The next section includes some ideas of how we can change the dialog, by arriving at some consensus of how to proceed. I would like to see the country share a Unifying Political Philosophy, a framework that brings us together to work on issues. That same framework might also help all of us be a lot more positive about the country, its people, its history, and its success. Wouldn't it feel good (OMG I am talking about feelings here) to look out at today's windy rainy day and remember that yesterday it was sunny and will be again in a couple of days from now instead of just hating the rain. We both might be a little more pleasant with that attitude. We might even be able to work together.

"If we look back to the riots and tumults which at various times have happened in England, we shall find that they did not proceed from the want of a government, but that government was itself the generating cause; instead of consolidating society, it divided it; it deprived it of its natural cohesion, and engendered discontent and disorder which otherwise would not have existed."

Thomas Paine,
THE RIGHTS OF MAN, 1791

8

LET'S WRAP UP
BY LOOKING AT HOW TO GET AT SOLUTIONS.

MELODY, IN YOUR comments, in conversations of how to remedy problems in America, you exert a strong belief that the Federal Government offers the best chance of solutions. You want legislators to pass legislation. You point to the history of the Federal Government fighting the Civil War to end slavery. Let us add other Federal Government successes. The New Deal helped cushion the pain of the Great Depression but didn't end it. The American policy and military have kept the homeland combat free since the War of 1812. The Voting Rights Act of the 1960s helped tear down artificial barriers to voting. It mandated that all races vote under the same rules. Antitrust legislation leveled the playing field for business. The Federal Government has a role in the country, but it is grown way beyond the role defined in the Constitution. For the last five decades, the Federal government has slowly usurped the responsibility of states to their citizens, parents to their children, and worst of all, citizens responsibility to themselves.

That growth is hurting the economy, the society, and many of the people it proclaims to be saving. Any action that discourages a citizen from working as hard as possible to help themselves is damaging. Any institution that dissuades citizens from exercising their creative and innovative skills only ensures problems do not get solved. It robs the country of millions of problem-solving brains. (One great example is the top-down directive in education from the U.S. Department Of Education. In the quest for federal dollars, local educators are directed into curriculum and testing that in many cases does not fit the needs of students or the community. Teacher innovation is lost to administrative tasking. Children suffer, the community suffers, and teachers burn out.)

The Constitution laid out a limited role for the Federal Government. It was to secure the borders, administer foreign tariffs, manage international affairs, provide for the nation's security, coordinate, and mediate between the states and most of all guarantee the individual rights of the citizens. The states agreed that the Federal Government could coordinate transportation since much of it is interstate. The primary power in government was reserved to the people and their elected representatives. Government closest to the citizens, local, then county, then state is best informed to support the collective needs that the citizens cannot better do for themselves. This is really important as the vast majority of us <u>are</u> really capable of **directing our own lives.**

But we have allowed the Federal Government to become involved in our lives to the degree that when states or individuals push back, seeking their rightful place, the media considers them radical. When the courts rule to push policy back to the elected representatives and the people, they are chastised, hounded as anti-people. Is it any wonder that many citizens are less motivated, less committed to their personal and family success when the average American now works about four months each year just to pay their taxes? That's one of every three workdays taken from each of us. Remember all we really have is our time and one third of our time is taken by government.

And government has become the driver of its own future. The

departments have evolved into bloated bureaucracies whose primary goal is **to just be**. To exist, they need to convince congress that they are tackling critical problems. Let's take the Department of Environmental Conservation as an example. They evolved from protecting the outdoors from damaging pesticides, water pollution issues and environmental cleanup to stopping climate change. In order to exist, they have become the source for the very data on issues that they want to tackle. In 1990 they predicted a global temperature increase of .3C per decade. Actual temperature rise has been about half of that, or about what it has been for preceding decades. They predicted world mean temperature would rise by 1C by 2025, but to date, the actual is about .4C. We aren't disputing warming exists, but hundred-year, thousand year and ten thousand historic temperature year cycles exist. The short-term predictions so far have been way off. A more accurate look at temperature change would be to compare them to historic cycles, not to what is happening right now. But to those who are terrified of global warming, these facts are irrelevant. And educational institutions and government stoke those fears. Only a day ago I was watching an interview with a really grounded environmentalist, a self-described progressive, who pointed out that issues like global warming are not resonating with lower income people. He saw the extreme screaming of many global warming activists as the ultimate white privilege and suggested a real change in the narrative; one that engaged all citizens in how their efforts on behalf of the environment created more opportunity and more good paying jobs. Real change needs to engage all of us.

In 2009, the EPA predicted an ice-free Arctic within six years, then revised it to fifteen years. In reality, the ice continues to fluctuate, but on average there has been little decrease. I believe the Arctic is warming and there will be less ice. We need to reduce man's impact and in the United States we are. But remember, that only a few thousand years ago the arctic was a temperate rain forest filled with animals, ferns, and freshwater lakes. Men were carrying spears.

The government predicted temperature rise would fuel wildfires, and there have been more dangerous fires, but most foresters believe that the problem is not only warming, but that we no longer manage forests allowing masses of fuel to accumulate. Heaven help a forester who wants to cut trees. The recently passed infrastructure act includes millions to begin clearing excess fuel from our forests. In California last year, in one forest, interlocking political issues eliminated all but 13 days of fuel mitigation. On days that burns could be held, air pollution laws kept foresters from controlled burning. There is no compromise. We continue to build homes in those forests increasing the financial damage of each fire. Man exposing their wealth to increased risk and then expecting the government to mitigate.

Especially in the Southwest, prolonged droughts are recorded every century. We are in one now and it is brutal, with vegetation, animals and man all affected. A century ago, the population of the west was 15% of what it is now, and water demands minimal.

The point is that this same department created administrative policy based on those estimates and have stubbornly refused to change them even when faced with conflicting data. We are not arguing that protecting the environment is not important, only that the size, shape, funding, and policies of a department should be directed by congress and should be based on real data. Each side to the debate only uses data that is favorable to their argument. When was the last major meeting of people from the environmental movement, government scientists, fossil fuel industry, energy distribution experts, developers, and policy makers? Did anyone listen?

How crazy is it for the Secretary of Energy to hold a press conference stating that curtailing American fossil energy production is critical to saving the world while her boss is calling authoritarian leaders in Iran, Venezuela, Russia, and Saudi Arabia, begging them to produce more oil? The price of oil has exploded. Half of the 2022 inflation is energy related.

Cleaner energy is possible, but the path our Federal Government has chosen is not sustainable. You cannot shift away from one critical technology, one that powers our lives, until another is ready to fill the void. We all remember the fiasco of switching water sources in Flint, Michigan. Realistic evolution created by market forces are needed. Government blundering in the name of correctness solves no problems, <u>ever</u>. Ask the less fortunate trying to buy gas to get to work. Ask the hospital workers in Ukraine who now work only in the basement because the upper floors of the hospitals have been demolished.

Public trust in government is shaky and it should be. The COVID phenomenon is another great example of a Federal Department's pronouncements on shaky ground. In the beginning we were told to get a COVID shot, to be protected from the virus. Then two shots to be protected, then add a booster. We were told that just like vaccines stopped measles, mumps, chickenpox and most importantly, polio, the COVID vaccine would protect us. But it didn't and the Department knew that it wasn't working as predicted within months. (In Britain, they estimate that 80% of COVID deaths in 2021 were among the fully vaccinated.) So, the message changed to 'shots will keep COVID from overwhelming the hospitals.' Then the message changed again to 'we won't get as sick.' The Department proclaimed that COVID on surfaces was a major cause of spread. We needed to sterilize anything we touched. The CDC knew within months that COVID's life on most surfaces was seconds and that there was little chance of major spread from touching anything. But as of this writing, they have not updated their formal advisories on how it is spread.

Mask messaging went from, not needed, to cloth masking will help, to cloth masks don't help so we need medical masks, to we need N95 masks, to they aren't very effective anyway, to oops let's mask up again. All of this was driven by government-initiated media. We were to avoid COVID at all costs, but it has been the spread of Omicron COVID that has led to mass exposure and finally to approaching herd immunity. To drive the Federal Government's confused message, it openly built an advertising campaign to instill fear. That fear has driven yet another wedge into society. Unreasonable fear like the woman at Costco who hysterically screamed, "get away from me," and threw her armful of fresh vegetables at a man who stepped in front of her to pick up some lettuce. Fear that has kept schools closed and driven teachers' unions to defy school district efforts to curtail masking among kids. Children who are being traumatized and learning disabled by masks and isolation. Keeping teachers safe is critical, but how we went about it created a national mental health crisis. This is a new disease, and the Federal CDC is learning more every day. But their credibility would have been greater and their ability to engage the public better if they had started with caution and not harsh actions. Fear is a critical response to danger, but it is a terrible foundation for learning.

The states that avoided mass business shutdowns have the exact same COVID history as those who killed off 20% or more of their small businesses with restrictions. The illness, hospitalization and death statistics are statistically the same.

Here again, look at damaging slogans and definitions. The Department constantly talks about vaccine efficacy. EFFICACY means how it performs under ideal lab conditions. They need to talk about effectiveness; that is how it works in the real world. We trusted the CDC because of the history and performance of, for example, the polio vaccine which wiped the disease out of American life. But the Department now predicts that we may need the COVID vaccine forever. Or maybe not at all. And the result: confusion and fear. After a year, about 15% of kids between five and fifteen are vaccinated, with no change in rates of serious illness.

But some of us are so fearful of COVID that we have demanded vaccination for under five kids, even though there is less risk of serious illness among this group than from the flu. The Federal Government spends hundreds of millions more, all borrowed, and Pfizer grows richer.

In the 1930's the Department of Health was deeply concerned about the long-term effects of sexual diseases on humans, especially as the nation looked to be slowly slipping into a new world at war. They deliberately refused to treat black citizens for sexually transmitted diseases, allowing them to die just to watch the progression of the sickness. The President Wilson era of prejudice and racism made those people unimportant. Government failure is not new.

The Federal Government has proclaimed that eating eggs is terrible for you, and after studying it, that eating eggs is good. Barbequing red meat will cause cancer, oops, we were wrong. The good food pyramid was taught for 30 years, only to be called unhealthy by the Federal Government. The polar bear would be extinct by 2020, but populations are the same as when that prediction was made. The Federal Government has rolled out literally dozens of restrictions on business over the last 50 years to level the workplace playing field, but there remain huge differences. Why? Because the regulations clashed with the motivations of Natural Americans rather than promote them. Government is not all bad, but its history is not very good at solving social or economic issues and the public has a right to question it. **You own you.**

On an international scale, the world is learning not to trust America's government. The same trust issues with our government overseas are now being seen among citizens. Are the foreign trust issues valid? When President Nixon negotiated the Paris Peace Accords to end the Vietnam War, he guaranteed South Vietnam that if the North did not honor its commitments to a negotiated peace, the United States would use American airpower to protect the South. But one Senator, a freshman from Delaware used his

'Senatorial hold power' to block funding to live up to that promise and the South was conquered by North Vietnam and their allies, China, and Russia, losing more troops in the final battle than the US lost in the entire war.

In Afghanistan the US spent 20 years helping the country modernize, telling its people, especially the women that their educational efforts would lead to a modern successful life and then we walked away. We built and tolerated a corrupt Afghan government. It collapsed in days when it turned out that many of the army units we paid to develop had only half the troops we were paying for. The rest of the money went into greedy pockets and ended up in banks all over the world. A small minority of the population conquered the majority who thought their military would protect the progress. Afghans were never prepared to fight to protect their new rights themselves, the government with U.S. money would take care of their security.

When Ukraine separated from Russia at the collapse of the Soviet Union it instantly became the third leading nuclear power in the world. Soviet nuclear weapons on Ukrainian soil numbered in the thousands. Russia and the US guaranteed Ukraine's independence if they would give up their stockpile of nuclear weapons. Russia agreed to protect their independence if they gave up those weapons. They didn't trust the Russians, but with America's guarantee Ukraine agreed. We are helping Ukraine in a war of survival, but we are a long way from guaranteeing its independence as promised. We promised to guarantee their non-nuclear future, one in which they were terrified of Russia. Russia lied to them. Now look.

Russia feels surrounded by newly minted NATO nations from the old Soviet Union. Those new states are all rightfully terrified of Russia as the war in Ukraine has proven. Their joining NATO was to secure their independence, and the American involvement in NATO was the most important guarantee. Watching the US shrink from its other commitments emboldens Russia. Are we stepping up to those commitments now? It appears that we are, but the war is only months old, and America's politicians often have short memories. The last president pressed Europe to pay their fair share of NATO costs, and they refused. The media vilified that president as anti-European. But today Germany has tripled their defense spending and the other NATO members are for the first time living up to their commitment to invest 2% of their gross national product to protect themselves and NATO.

We make these observations, because the US has been unable or unwilling to live up to the commitments it has made to many of its own citizens. The country's internal conflicts have, over and over, led to a failure to deliver, failure to meet past promises. Getting hundreds of thousands of federal bureaucrats in line with what Americans really want has failed. Remember the economist Milton Friedman's warning to judge policies and programs by their results, rather than their intentions.

The Secretary of Transportation was asked, "How are lower income people, driving old cars that only get ten miles to the gallon, supposed to cope with exploding gas prices?" His answer, "They should buy an electric car." This is wrong on so many levels. First, a citizen driving a twenty-year-old Ford probably does not have the resources to go out and buy an $80,000 car. Second, as previously noted, the heads of Toyota and of Tesla both looked at the huge infrastructure bill passed last year and warned, "We are nowhere ready to jettison gas-powered vehicles." Why, the electric grid is already struggling to cope with the increased demand of electric cars in some areas and the national grid will not be able to charge cars and trucks, (even if only 50% of the current gas-powered fleet converts), for decades. In rural America the grid may never support electric vehicles. But the government's policy is to go electric. Last year British Columbia taught us what that might look at. On one holiday weekend where people from the southern metropolitan area drove north to the B.C. Parks region, those with electric vehicles had to wait for hours to recharge enough drive home. Some were stuck for days. In a power outage they would all be stuck. But the B.C. government continues to promote electric.

Let's look at electric power as a cure-all for the environment. First, batteries do not make electricity. They either store electricity made elsewhere from coal, gas, solar, waterpower, wind power, or uranium or they are charged by gas or diesel-powered generators. The minerals needed to make these batteries include, lithium, manganese, silver oxide or zinc and carbon to store electricity chemically. There are other technical combinations in use. They are all toxic and need to be mined. Other technologies for proposed batteries include other toxic and difficult to produce minerals and rare earths. Most of these come from China and Russia because in America **mining is bad.**

To make one electric car auto battery, you need to process 25,000 pounds of brine for lithium, 30,000 pounds of ore for cobalt, 5,000 pounds of ore for nickel, and 25,000 pounds of ore for copper. Overall, that represents digging up about 500,000 pounds of earth and processing it to make one battery. The analyst, Susan K. Munson Bliesner points out that Einstein's famous formula for energy, "E=MC2 tells us that it takes the same amount of energy to move a five-thousand-pound gasoline-driven automobile a mile as it does an electric one."

(Windmills, solar panels, and other green generating technologies also use toxic materials and very dirty manufacturing techniques to build them. When they fail, they cannot be recycled. By some evaluations there is more environmentally damaging release from the production, transportation, installation, and replacement of these technologies than from natural gas generation. Wind power today is generating only 25% of the power promised ten years ago.)

We all need to be a bit more skeptical of government. Far from solving many problems that it defines; it only perpetuates them. It offers feel-good ideas with few real hard documented solutions.

Imagine how much progress we could make if all of our citizens were engaged; motivated to find new cleaner technology, or that makes fossil fuels environmentally acceptable. But a lot of citizens aren't really participating in the economy at all; many have accepted sloganeering from special interests instead of figuring out how to become rich by improving America's energy technology. To many, those who refuse to toe the line on environmental issues are out to destroy the world, heretics. But they are not.

Much of our society, by most polling numbers more than 60%, do not trust government to solve problems. Part of that distrust is rooted in the bureaucracy's need to perpetuate itself by either never really solving what it is working on or worse, by redefining man's relationship with man to find new problems that only government can solve. Every year we pile law on top of law, regulation on top of regulation, and policy on top of policy and none seem to ever go away. In the 1950s a budget bill in Congress might have been 300 pages. The budget bill of 2022 was 2,700 pages, and it was voted on before members of Congress or their staff could read it. It wasn't created by elected representatives, but by staffers directed by the federal departments. Life gets more complex, and man is trusted less to make good decisions to take care of themselves. How many of us still need government to tell us that smoking is bad for us, or that drinking to excess is dangerous, or that we should use seatbelts. But the departments that were tasked with working on those issues, still exist.

We are closest to government officials in our hometown. Whether you are concerned about the environment, or economy, or civil-rights, or healthcare, or any other issue, that is where you personally can have the greatest impact. (Conservatives have a terrible habit of not participating in local elections and it really costs them.) You can support candidates, vote, or run for office yourself. The same is true for county or statewide issues. Or you can band together and attack the issues with like-minded associates. There is a good chance that it will be solved more quickly, more successfully and for a lot less invested wealth (time=money). You and your local fellow citizens are closest to the problems, know the players, and can craft the most direct and meaningful solution. Of course, if that solution also requires an investment, you must also figure out how to pay for it. Gather a group of people together and form a company to grow rich while solving problems.

But for too long we comfortably sit in our bubbles, liking Facebook posts we agree with and slamming those we disagree with while we wait for government to solve everything. You own you; you control your time; you can move beyond today.

One thing about getting directly involved, it will show that some problems are rooted in society, some even in Natural Law, most involving man who is not perfect, and your efforts will not be a lot different than those of the founding fathers. Race, jobs, family economic security, education, immigration, mitigating natural disaster, and international conflict were all problems when the nation was founded and are still problems now. But **keep working at it** even though you know that there is no such thing as perfection among humans. We must keep working at it. But do not be so set in your efforts that you leave out others who might have a different idea on solving the problem. You own you, offer a hand to those who need help and together you can probably make that one degree of change that when combined with others, moves the needle. Recognize as I have that perfection is not possible if for no other reason than society's values change over time. What looks like perfection today will look like part of a problem in a few decades. But we can all make things a little better, with commitment and **patience.**

Liberal views do shine a light on many of the problems in our society. President Andrew Jackson openly promoted greater success of the Common Man. He was probably America's first Liberal President, even though today many progressives would erase him.

Like so many, he was a flawed man. His ideas are still one of the foundations of the progressive movement.

Melody, if we can stop the name calling and bickering, the sloganeering and redefining of basic values, we can make more progress with a lot less effort. Conservatives who oppose government social programs are not uncaring as many of your peers may think. They just have watched people's hopes diminish as government trying what it was never created to do spins its wheels. Like Natural Americans, we can be a Natural Society, creating more wealth for more people with a lot less effort. We need to add thinking and knowledge to feeling and move from political philosophies that divide to something that brings us together.

We submit that what the country needs most is a **unifying philosophy of success**. The vast majority of us see <u>common problems</u>. But not all. Unequal status is part of a historic system that can raise up everyone, but racism isn't. We need to agree on common terms and definitions, and then solutions. We're not talking about special interest issues that only affect a few. (This year there are 12,000 different special interest groups who employ political lobbyists in America.) We're talking about the big picture here. The nation needs to pick two or three agreed upon problems at a time and then lay out a strategy to tackle them. Imagine if you funneled just a third of the money these special interest groups demand into cancer research. Do you think that we might finally get our hands around this scourge?

There will be screaming and hollering as we focus more energy and wealth on fewer issues. Every one of us **is** important. Natural Americans, working hard, creating their own wealth, investing that wealth on issues where they find common concerns with others, are far more capable of actually solving problems than government. Unleash those who for years have been led to believe that they are victims and cannot succeed on their own. Let them start at the bottom, perform, and move up. Some will not succeed on their own. Let them appeal to benefactors with similar backgrounds and interests for support. Re-channel the resources government pours into <u>victim and disadvantaged forever</u> programs into programs that both encourage and demand success. Take the money away from government; direct it into foundations or organizations where the investors manage the funds to get results.

Instead of criticizing those with great wealth, encourage them to invest it in societal needs and then celebrate what they are doing.

For years my life was twisted by a relationship with an alcoholic. I tried everything to help. After all, this old white guy grew up in an environment where men were supposed to take care of their families and were expected to fix things. Rehab and meetings and counseling did nothing except push me to try something more. Each new effort was met by genuine appreciation but no real improvement. The alcoholic's personal circle, government and the media reinforced that alcoholism is a disease, they were a victim. Anyone who has lived with an addict or alcoholic knows that nothing will get better until the afflicted person makes a decision to fix the problem. But it is hard, really hard to turn loose. By the time I finally had enough and cut the ties, I was as sick as the alcoholic, but it was the sickness of codependence.

No nation offers more opportunity than America. Those who believe in God believe that its creation was divine. It is one of only a handful of nations that has never had a monarch or dictator or strong man as leader. Its government exists to protect the liberty and opportunity of the individual. It is better, not perfect. It is a remarkable country; one that almost everyone can succeed in. But it is mired in **codependence.** We reinforce that some people cannot succeed, that hurdles not of their own making limit people's success. We need to change that to reinforcing the opportunity of every person to become a Natural American, to succeed, to create as much wealth as possible with as little work as possible. We need to help people see that hurdles are different than barriers. But they need to do it honorably without hurting fellow Americans. We need to stop the codependence, and the selfishness of government agencies and special interest groups who succeed only because they perpetuate ongoing problems and victims.

We need to accept that there will always be people who are inconsiderate, selfish, and difficult with warped views and values. They have the legal right to those opinions. Our goal should be to ensure that fewer and fewer people fall into this trap. Some of these people have legitimate grievances, but because of how they act out, we never listen to them. We need to <u>replace envy with pride in personal achievement</u> and improved lives as we make the pie bigger.

We need to take the responsibility for success, for public safety, for environmental well-being away from those whose own success depends on those issues continuing. We need to liberate the power of Natural Americans. We need to reembrace the promise of a nation that was created around one word, one idea, **liberty.**

Here are some thoughts on what might make up the proposed **unifying political philosophy of success.**

First for any philosophy to succeed it needs to recognize and respect natural law. Proposing anything that goes against natural law, like the drive to create wealth with as little effort as possible is doomed to fail.

The founding fathers gave us a remarkable Constitution that encourages personal achievement while calling out that we cannot harm others. Any philosophy needs to follow the Constitution, not find ways around it. Should we find new needs, we can amend that document. The legal system, under our Constitution does not exist to solve societal problems; that is the responsibility of the people and elected officials. The courts need to return to the concept of adjudicating whether a situation falls under legally passed laws, laws that are constitutional, and we need to demand that our elected leaders address societal ills, but in a way that protects the rights of all.

We need to quit calling the other side names. For us to really solve problems we need each other's help. This requires us to arrive at common definitions: for example, examine police brutality which is often defined by what percentage of arrests are by race, and consider examining what percentage of arrests are made based on percentages of criminal acts. In one of my fictional thrillers, I note a police department organization that kept track of drunk Latin Americans they "scraped off the highway," every payday. The scene came from an actual visit to a police station. This is wrong and needs to be addressed, as does the drinking and driving problem it refers to, and the definition of alcohol problems as a racial issue.

We need to unfriend those who enflame each other with sloganeering and friend those who offer real ideas on how personal responsibility can improve lives.

Consistent with above, we need to seek out others or groups who can help all citizens build on individual pride in achievement, even entry level, building confidence. Children's activities that reward participation instead of achievement and pride in success need revising. It is okay to feel bad, to fail and use that to be better, to learn, do better.

We should seriously look at who we support for public office. Political sloganeering, based on political litmus tests, for example labeling a Republican who doesn't vote as we might like on an issue or two as RINOs, only further divides us. People like Joe Mansion who do not ascribe to uber liberal policies are not "closet Republicans" but rather could be considered as trying to find common ground. (He is blasted by the majority of Democratic congressmen who come from just ten states out of fifty, all very liberal.) Quit letting others tell us how we should vote and get involved in Party platform issues.

With better legislators, we can demand that the government and its agencies quit lobbying congress, quit promoting what the bureaucrats want. Government should only be doing what the people cannot do for themselves. We need to elect those who listen to all of us and not just pander to special interest. It should be criminal for government to present inaccurate information, and to use it to promote policy. Demand Congress and legislatures make government an honest source of information. At the same time demand that Congress enact legislation that prohibits elected officials from profiting from legislation or policy that they influence. It should infuriate all of us when elected officials invest in medical companies just before they pass pandemic legislation. None of us should accept elected officials buying defense stocks just before military budgets are changed.

We need to ask how a President who comes into office with a net worth of $500,000 is worth $50,000,000 four years after leaving office and almost ten times that ten years later.

With better legislators we can demand that government focuses on the budgets of the citizens and wise use of their tax dollars. Government can use competitive bidding for most goods and services and competitive proposals for innovative needs. How crazy is it that only the Federal Government is prohibited from competitively sourcing lifesaving drugs? Government must stop picking winners and losers.

We should consider banning all hyphenated descriptions of American citizens from the law. We should honor Natural Americans of every race and religion by referring simply to them as men or women or citizens. (Sorry, we understand that some struggle with that description of their mind/body connection, but I grew up with only two sexes. I also grew up with the knowledge that liberty meant that others believed differently. Those who feel otherwise are free to define themselves, they own themselves. Just as important, they should not live in fear.)

People can be proud of their heritage, of where they came from, without emphasizing that somehow, they are different from, better or worse, than others. Refocus K-12 education on core subjects including civics. Give parents some economic power to motivate schools to perform, or to move their children if they don't. Of all the issues facing disadvantaged families trapped in poor performing schools, none is more wrong than their children not having the opportunity to relocate their children as wealthier parents can do. Pay good teachers more and great teachers a lot more. Remove the obstacles to kicking out our lousy teachers. Encourage students, outside the classroom, to read materials that can energize personal or family pride and pride in heritage. But keep race out of the classroom. Consider, at least consider, a whole new model for education, one that first prepares children for citizenship and then for careers or higher education. A system where all parents have confidence in their child's education because they chose the path.

Let's rejoice in the creation of personal success, even wealth, of individuals. While we will never eliminate human foibles such as envy, jealousy, and anger, we can focus our collective energy on making the pie bigger for everyone. Let's consider adopting those who really make life more successful and better as our influencers instead of what, for sake of a better example, old Christian teachings called false prophets. We can reject false choices. Let's embrace opportunity instead of envy. Let's embrace higher success for all instead of equality.

The brave and incredibly talented Russian writer, Aleksandr Solzhenitsyn, the man who blew the whistle on the excesses and brutality of the Communist government of Russia explained the choice clearly. **"Liberty, by its very nature, undermines social equality, and equality suppresses liberty-for how else could it be attained?"**

Let's pick three problems and work on them together. Educational achievement and the application of what is learned by teaching people how to think would be a good start. Some who are deeply entrenched in keeping the current educational model will be hurt. Don't abandon feeling, but as you noted in the survey, it is not a strong basis for action.

For those of faith, virtually every faith calls out behaviors, like the Ten Commandments, that outline relationships with our fellow man. Why some are concerned that others are people of faith makes no sense. At the same time, people of faith should be free to promote it, but not to demand that others believe the same thing. If people choose to live their faith, and that gives them strength, encourage that. Those without faith are free to find similar guidelines. Do no harm to fellow citizens.

Melody, I am sure that you have questions about the positions and documentation in this book. That is perfect. Do your own research. Engage beyond your immediate circle. Where you arrive at different thoughts, I am happy; discuss them not only with your peers but those on the other side. We share similar goals. You are not our enemy, and we are not yours. We are free to disagree and then work together in a country that was conceived on **liberty.** The founding fathers embraced the arguments in Thomas Paine's COMMON SENSE. They created a remarkable nation, with a remarkable economic model, and have preserved it through historical struggle and legal challenge. What the founders built was copied all over the world, but never as successfully.

Smile at your friends who come from advantaged backgrounds, who themselves have known little want and feel guilty about that. Work with them to create a bigger pie, a more diverse pie, that creates opportunity for people to thrive instead of surviving. After all, guilt is just one of the feelings that is not a strong foundation for decision making.

Re-label those you have called victims in the past as future political and economic contributors and then encourage them to succeed.

The **COMMON SENSE of the mid 1770's** makes even more sense today. Embrace this nation. Replace chants like 'Black Lives Matter,' and 'Let's Go Brandon,' with 'We're Natural Americans.' This country that has demonstrated its ability to support its citizens, but not as successfully as it might have if government hadn't diluted the tools and lessons of the founding fathers. Trusting in America's strengths is powerful, while recognizing that it can still be better, is **STILL COMMON SENSE.**

AFTERWORD

I hope that **STILL COMMON SENSE,** has given you a fact-based justification for American exceptionalism; not perfection, but an economy, culture, history, and legal system that is always improving. One of the nation's most important characteristics is the use of inequality and empathy in each generation to improve their personal lives and that of all Americans.

STILL COMMON SENSE is complex, with integrated discussions across all four topics. Perhaps the topics and conclusions will be difficult to explain to others. (It took me a full year just to write the book.) Early readers of the book made clear that its content and themes are something that they would like to share with children and grandchildren, with employees, and with others who know things can be better but aren't quite sure how to help make that happen.

With that in mind, I wrote **AWAKE – We're Not So Divided**, a fictional story that takes Rodger and Melody into a real-world situation. **AWAKE** is about 80 pages, written in an easy to read and digest style. It touches on economy, history, culture, and legal issues, but in a conversational way. It is the perfect format for sharing the message of **STILL COMMON SENSE** with those you would like to reach. It doesn't require research, isn't confrontational or accusatory, and because of its length, works for those who get their news in snippets from electronic media. Early readers say that it's a fun read.

AWAKE is very inexpensive and available in eBook and paperback from Amazon, Barnes & Noble and in multi-book packages directly from *rodgercarlyle.com*. The multi-packs are perfect for those who would like to reach four or five grandchildren or a thousand employees. For those concerned about the lack of real civics education in schools, **AWAKE** might be used to counter the victim centered curriculum currently being taught in many American schools.

For a synopsis, go to *rodgercarlyle.com* and click on **AWAKE**. You can order the Amazon or Barnes & Noble versions through my website, or the multi-pack booklets directly.

Thank you,

Rodger

ABOUT THE AUTHOR

RODGER CARLYLE is a storyteller who draws on an enormous personal library of experiences. An adventurer, political strategist, and ghostwriter whose love of flying began in the Navy, his experiences stretch from New York to Los Angeles, from Amsterdam to Khabarovsk in the Russian Far East, and from Canada into Latin America.

Through his passion for research, he treasures finding those events that are ignored or covered up by the powerful when some strategy or plan goes completely to hell. From there, he creates a fictional adventure narrative that tells a more complete story.

Rodger is comfortable in black tie urban settings, but he is never happier than in the wilderness. He has faced down muggers in San Francisco, intimidation by the Russian Mafia, and charging grizzly bears. Most of his stories take his readers to places they will never visit. He likes to think that he is there with them.

Visit Rodger Carlyle's website at www.rodgercarlyle.com
Goodreads Author Rodger Carlyle
Amazon Author Rodger Carlyle